BIRMINGHAM COLLEGE OF FOOD, TOURISM & CREATIVE STUDIES
COLLEGE LIBRARY, SUMMER ROW
BIRMINGHAM B3 1JB
Tel: (0121) 243 0055

Pe

DATE OF RETURN		
0 6 JUN 2007	5 DEC 2008	
	1 9 JAN 2009	
2 9 OCT 2007	8 MAR 2009	
− 6 DEC 2007		
	24 NOV 2010	
2 5 JAN 2008		
1 0 OCT 2003		
− 7 NOV 2008		

Books <u>must</u> be returned by the last date stamped
or further loans may not be permitted

Torben Juul Andersen

Editor

Perspectives on Strategic Risk Management

Copenhagen Business School Press

Perspectives on Strategic Risk Management
© Copenhagen Business School Press
Printed in Denmark by Narayana Press, Gylling
Cover design by Morten Højmark
1. edition 2006

ISBN 87-630-0183-7

Distribution:

Scandinavia
DJØF/DBK, Mimersvej 4
DK-4600 Køge, Denmark
Phone: +45 3269 7788, fax: +45 3269 7789

North America
Copenhagen Business School Press
Books International Inc.
P.O. Box 605
Herndon, VA 20172-0605, USA
Phone: +1 703 661 1500, fax: +1 703 661 1501

Rest of the World
Marston Book Services, P.O. Box 269
Abingdon, Oxfordshire, OX14 4YN, UK
Phone: +44 (0) 1235 465500, fax: +44 (0) 1235 465555
E-mail Direct Customers: direct.order@marston.co.uk
E-mail Booksellers: trade.order@marston.co.uk

Table of Contents

Table of Contents

Introduction/Preface

The international business environment is becoming increasingly turbulent as innovations continue to mold competition, political changes influence market relations, and environmental hazards expose the economic infrastructure while financial markets are as erratic as ever. Across industries competition is characterized by increased specialization, complexity, and faster and frequent change, all reflective of 'hypercompetitive' conditions that challenge the strategic resolve of commercial enterprise. At the same time society is facing systemic economic and political risks across interacting global markets, worldwide climatic changes, and threats of international terrorism. This accentuates the need for effective strategic risk management practices to deal with these phenomena both at corporate management and public policy levels.

Conducting business in global markets exposes the corporation to many risks and exogenous influences that are beyond managerial control but also represents new strategic opportunities. Hence, strategic risk management is focused on the elimination of downside risk while attempting to optimize economic returns from alternative business initiatives under uncertain market conditions. This is a daunting task but one that must be pursued with vigor because it is the essential driver of competitive advantage under global competition. It seems pretty clear that corporate risk management capabilities are essential to limit the adverse economic effects from market volatility and other exogenous influences thereby facilitating economic growth to the benefit of the general public. While corporate risk management capabilities are essential for economic wealth creation, public policy also plays an important role by supporting a reliable economic infrastructure in politically stable societies.

Large multinational corporations, small-to-medium sized businesses, and the communities in which they operate are exposed to many exogenous risk factors outside the control of executives and policy makers. These exposures span a variety of influences ranging from commodity and financial market prices, macroeconomic conditions, operational disruptions, human error and misconduct, technological jumps, competitive moves, socio-political events, man-made disasters, natural hazards, etc. Each of these risk areas are addressed through rather disparate approaches of financial risk modeling, multinational exposure management, actuarial science, reinsurance, risk financing, business continuity planning, strategy analysis, risk mitigation, catastrophe preparedness, etc., often promoted within relatively narrow academic disciplines.

Some inroads to integrate these diverse approaches have been made by introducing formal risk management practices initially geared to the financial sector and subsequently extended into enterprise-wide approaches. Many of these managerially oriented efforts have been practitioner driven rather than spurned by an academic drive. This strategic risk management challenge goes beyond an ability to manage price fluctuations, financial exposures, and insurance risks. Some of the most essential corporate exposures frequently deal with complex operational, competitive, and strategic risks that are hard to quantify. Hence, there is a need to develop insights beyond the conventional scope of risk management and identify effective strategy processes that enable organizations to respond better under the new environmental reality.

In theory, risk management starts with the identification of significant factors that expose economic assets and business activities not unlike the consideration of strengths, weaknesses, opportunities, and threats in strategy analysis. Once these factors are identified the vulnerability to the various risks can be analyzed and the potential economic effects determined. Measures of the impact on asset values and economic performance provide a basis to analyze potential benefits from different risk mitigation efforts and the need for risk-transfer and financing arrangements. Whereas this normative description is relatively well developed, there is a need to better understand how the interaction between the diverse exposures can be effectively managed. Many important risks are hard to quantify as they bound in human behaviors, competitive moves, technological changes, product and process innovations, political events, etc. While formal control systems enable the monitoring of these types of exposures their effective handling may to a large extent depend on informal adaptive strategy processes that enhance organizational responsiveness.

Many approaches and methodologies have been introduced to deal more systematically with the diverse exposures in more integrative ways. Over the past decade, the banking industry has developed quite sophisticated value-at-risk models to assess interacting influences of financial prices and stipulate profiles for the associated market exposures of financial institutions. The economic exposures of multinational enterprises have similarly been analyzed from the perspective of interacting influences of macroeconomic indicators over time. Elements of these approaches have been adopted in enterprise risk management models considering a wider range of risks and their possible interactions. However, this diversity of approaches spans from extremely data rich value-at-risk calculations of market exposures to assessments of firm-specific strategic exposures with relatively poor data support. Hence, it is appropriate to consider how these partial approaches can be incorporated into the overall strategic risk management process. Central elements of the strategic management process comprise risk management considerations in conjunction with planning discussions, environmental analyses, contingency plans, strategic controls, etc. The ability to respond to changing conditions is also influenced by the organization's decision structure and absorption of market intelligence, internal information exchange, and eventually the use of these insights to construe and execute suitable responsive actions.

A major purpose of this anthology is to inspire our thinking about integrative risk management approaches and further considerations of effective strategic risk management. To this end the book presents a collection of contemporary articles that discuss different aspects of the strategic risk management concept with an aim of inspiring new thoughts and creating a better understanding of this complex subject. The book collects ten articles that combine the perspectives of practitioners and academics with different involvements in the risk management issue.

The first chapter deals with the rather fundamental issue whether effective risk management has discernible effects on corporate performance. Fortunately, the data seem to support the notion that strategic risk management capabilities are important drivers of corporate value creation. In the second chapter, Torsten Andersen and Anette Terp give an excellent outline of how strategic risk analysis is perceived by a leading American insurance group and constitutes a prime example of current professional practice in the field. In chapter three Torben J. Andersen and Richard A. Bettis introduce a simple model of strategic adaptation effects based on the idea that effective risk management deals as much with exploitation of upside potential as the avoidance of downside losses. The adjacent simulation analysis illustrates how an ability to observe environmental change and respond to it can lead to higher average performance and lower performance risk at the same time.

Given the apparent importance of effective risk management practices, chapter four takes a closer look at how corporate executives deal with the strategic risk management concept. In this article, Peter W. Schrøder reports the results of a recent study analyzing the implementation of formal risk management practices among Danish corporations and discusses the impediments that seem to exist for their practical implementation. In the context of increasing risk consciousness, attention to operational risk factors, and formal requirements for risk reporting, Kim Klarskov Jeppesen presents a very timely analysis from the auditors' perspective in chapter five. The article emphasizes the need to consider internal processes and structural factors as influencers of the auditors' ability to handle major risks. Given the diverse applications of the strategic risk management concept it is highly relevant to consider how risk management approaches are conceived by different contributors in the field. In chapter 6, Per Henriksen and Thomas Uhlenfeldt presents the intriguing conclusions from a comparative study of predominant risk management frameworks. Interestingly, they conclude that effective risk management practices should relate to the very strategy formation process, an element that seems to be absent from the current risk management frameworks.

In view of the complexity of risk factors that expose multinational corporations, chapter 7 outlines an integrative risk management framework that considers various risk classes, including financial, casualty, catastrophe, operational, political, economic, as well as strategic risks, such as, new innovations, technology shifts, competitor moves, etc. Country risk assessments constitute an essential element of business evaluations in the multinational enterprise but these efforts are approached in many different ways. In chapter 8, Mikelle A. Calhoun presents an interesting and highly relevant analysis of the validity of different sovereign risk indices commonly used in international business. This research reaches the startling conclusion that the many seemingly differentiated risk indices are highly confluent, which questions their validity as useful risk measures. Risk exposures may apply to countries as well as to corporations and to this end chapter 9 introduces the risk management concept from a central government perspective. Governments and regional authorities often act as 'lenders of last resort' in connection with large catastrophie events whether related to natural hazards or man-made disaster events.

This article takes a look at how governments should deal with such essential societal risks particularly when the exposures reach catastrophic proportions.

The final article in chapter 10 presents an alternative perspective of the strategic risk management process by incorporating a real options analytical framework to deal with more firm-specific risks. The article theorizes how effective strategy formation processes may facilitate the creation of operational flexibilities and essential business opportunities (real options) and help decision makers utilize the embedded strategic flexibilities to enhance corporate performance. An empirical study seems to confirm some of the basic performance effects associated with a real options analytical framework.

It is hoped that this collection of articles will contribute with some new, relevant, and useful perspectives on the challenge associated with the management of risk exposures and thereby provide inspiration to practitioners and scholars alike in their efforts to develop more effective integrated strategic risk management practices.

Acknowledgements

Several people have been instrumental in the efforts to complete this book. I would like to thank Ole Wiberg, Managing Director of CBS Press, for his continued support to this project and Hanne Thorninger Ipsen, Project Manager, who was instrumental in the final editing of the book. Chris Eberhart of the American Chamber of Commerce kindly offered her support proofreading the manuscript. These contributions are truly appreciated.

Torben Juul Andersen
Frederiksberg
February 2006

CHAPTER 1

Performance Effects of Risk Management[1]

Torben Juul Andersen

There has been an exponential growth in outstanding derivative instruments in conjunction with a widespread promotion of enterprise risk management practices over the past decade. With an increasing risk management focus the essential question arises whether effective risk management practices have positive performance effects or should remain supported by anecdotal evidence. To address this issue, the article outlines an empirical study performed to test the relationships between risk management, financial leverage, and economic performance in a large cross-sectional sample.

Introduction

The use of global derivatives has grown exponentially and together with the emergence of new alternative risk-transfer instruments it has provided the basis for improved corporate risk management capabilities (Merton, 1995). As a consequence, corporations displaying effective risk management outcomes in the form of a stable earnings development may reduce their capital reserves as a buffer to shield against bankruptcy risk. A reduced need for capital reserves constitutes an opportunity to increase financial leverage, which in turn should reduce the average cost of capital. Effective risk management reduces variance in economic performance and thereby should lower the cost of funding for both equity and debt instruments. Lower cost of capital improves the economics of business propositions, which should lead to

---

[1] Parts of this article are based on Andersen, T. J. (2005). Global derivatives, risk management, and capital structure. Paper presented at the Business & Economics Society International Conference, Flagstaff, AZ, USA.

better economic performance. Or stated differently, effective risk management should eliminate adverse effects of downside risk events and extract extraordinary gains from upside potentials thus leading to superior performance outcomes. This study analyzes these relationships based on a comprehensive dataset comprised of more than 1400 corporations operating across different industries during the period 1996-2000. The study provides empirical support for the propositions that risk management is associated with higher financial leverage and economic performance after controlling for potentially confounding effects of organizational size, agency conflicts, and stock market valuation.

Global Derivatives

The explosive growth in the use of derivative instruments allows traders to hedge against price fluctuations and market participants can diversify various risk exposures among them by engaging in risk transfer arrangements (Rawls and Smithson, 1990; Merton, 1995). Risk management techniques developed in the financial industry have been widely adopted in business enterprise to deal with corporate exposures through integrated risk assessment techniques considering longer-term economic exposures (Eiteman, Stonehill and Moffett, 1994; Froot, 1999). Enterprise risk management has emerged as an integrative managerial approach considering market risks, environmental hazards, political risks, competitive risks, technology risks, etc., as they affect corporate performance (DeLoach, 2000; Lam, 2003). While financial derivatives exist for many traded assets, the management of firm-specific risk factors often depends on the adoption of flexible strategic management processes embedded in appropriate decision structures, information and communication systems, etc. Structural flexibilities should help the corporation mitigate adverse effects of longer term economic and competitive exposures associated with changes in demand conditions and factor prices (Allen and Pantzalis, 1996; Kogut and Kulatilaka, 1994).

Capital Structure and Risk Management

Modigliani and Miller (1958) argued that the value of the firm is independent of its capital structure under given conditions. One important condition was perfect capital markets, that is, no taxes, no transaction costs, and no bankruptcy costs. However, when interest expenses are tax deductible, corporate performance should be advantaged by higher financial leverage (Modigliani and Miller,

1963). In this situation, the optimal capital structure is supposedly determined by a trade-off between increased bankruptcy risk from higher debt load and tax advantage associated with debt. Furthermore, when managers know more about the investment opportunities than investors, the firm may prefer to use internal funds for good projects and only assume external debt to fund additional less attractive projects (Myers and Majluf, 1984). In this case, the relationship between financial leverage and economic performance may depend on the pool of good business opportunities and the availability of favorably priced debt. Hence, conventional finance theories do not provide clear answers to the relationship between financial leverage and economic performance.

In an analysis of capital structure decisions, Ward (1993) distinguished between business risk and financial risk. Business risk relates to adverse effects from environmental uncertainties and financial risk relates to exposures imposed by providers of external funds, i.e., lenders and investors. Corporations operating in environments with high business risk should assume low financial risk by decreasing leverage. Conversely, leverage is better in stable business environments where there is little need for a financial buffer. This argues for an inverse relationship between business risk and financial leverage, a phenomenon supported by empirical studies using different conceptualizations of business risk, such as, variance in sales growth (Thies and Klock, 1992) and volatility of demand (Chung, 1993).

Firms operating in markets with high business risk engage in innovative ventures to achieve superior performance and gain sustainable competitive advantage through deployment of valuable, rare, unsubstitutable, inimitable, firm specific-assets (Barney, 1991; D'Aveni, 1994). This in turn argues for lower leverage to maintain a financial buffer for development projects, i.e., lower financial leverage is likely to be associated with higher performance under hypercompetition. According to a transaction cost economics rationale, transaction costs are lower when they are carried out on the basis of standardized assets with low specificity while transaction costs are higher in the case of firm-specific assets. That is, the higher the asset specificity, the more economical internal hierarchical coordination should be compared to market clearance of transactions (Williamson, 1988, 1991). A higher equity base supports internal hierarchical control whereas external debt imposes market discipline on the organization. Consequently, equity should be the preferred source of financing when asset specificity is high (Harris and Raviv, 1991; Balakrishnan and Fox, 1993). In this set-up, lenders are the prime governance constituents as enforceable debt obligations make it difficult for indebted firms to engage in peripheral business activities. However, debt can also be too restrictive for firms operating in turbulent environments that need a high degree of strategic responsiveness. These arguments imply that firms operating under hypercompetitive conditions should reduce leverage to economize on transaction cost and engage in innovative ventures to increase responsiveness. These improved risk management capabilities might enable the corporation to manage business risk imposed by environmental uncertainty and thereby reduce the variability in corporate earnings.

Risk management may be important because some of the corporation's essential stakeholders are unable to diversify investments geared to maintain firm-specific relationships, e.g., in buyer and supplier relationships, business partnerships, employment contracts, etc. (Miller, 1998). From this perspective, the corporation needs capital reserves to maintain a financial cushion to shield against potential exogenous shocks and thereby assure key stakeholders that the corporation appears reliable and financially sound. From an 'insurative' view, insurance contracts constitute residual claims as well as equity funding shields against defined exogenous shocks, i.e., capital structure and risk management decisions are two sides of the same coin (Shimpi, 1999). The increased use of derivative instruments, risk-linked securities, contingent capital, etc., all serve to transfer risk that is beyond management control and thereby constitute sources of financial capital (Culp, 2002). As a consequence, the increased use of financial derivatives and alternative risk-transfer instruments should, everything else equal, reduce the need for capital reserves since they constitute direct substitutes for equity.

Hypotheses

Capital reserves provide a financial buffer to absorb the adverse economic impact of exogenous shocks, e.g., imposed by unexpected events. Use of derivatives and other risk-transfer instruments can help the corporation in reducing variability in periodic cash flows and reported earnings as they are affected by changing environmental conditions. To the extent this type of active risk management can lower the level of business risk it provides management with an opportunity to increase financial risk associated with a higher debt load (Ward, 1993). Hence, corporations that are able to impose effective risk management practices that reduce the volatility of corporate earnings diminish the need for capital reserves, i.e., effective risk management reduces the risk of bankruptcy and makes it possible to increase financial leverage (Miller and Modigliani, 1958, 1963). The reduced cost of capital deriving from lower bankruptcy risk makes debt financing of incremental business projects more favorable and thereby tends to increase leverage (Myers and Majluf, 1984). These rationales lead to the following hypothesis.

HYPOTHESIS 1: *Firms demonstrating effective risk management capabilities are associated with higher financial leverage.*

Effective risk management will dampen the volatility of corporate cash flows and thereby reduce the cost of potential financial distress, which in turn should reduce the average cost of capital. These effects will improve the debt capacity of the corporation and reduce the cost of alternative risk-transfer solutions thus diminishing the need for capital reserves. With improved credit worthiness, the funding available for favorable projects is readily extended thus making it more attractive to engage in good incremental business activities (Myers and Majluf, 1984). Hence, improved risk management capabilities tend to reduce under investment problems caused by debt overhang and allow the corporation to engage in positive net present value projects (Myers, 1984, Froot, Scharfstein and Stein, 1993, 1994). This argues for the following hypothesis.

HYPOTHESIS 2: *Firms demonstrating effective risk management capabilities are associated with higher economic performance.*

The subsequent section describes the empirical study devised to test the hypotheses.

Methodology

Data and Measures
The empirical study is based on a sample of large US corporations including Fortune 500 companies, Stern-Stewart Performance Top 1000 companies, and the 1000 largest companies in Compustat based on market capitalization. These sources identified a total of 1450 companies operating across four-digit SIC-code industries with

financial information available from Compustat. Economic performance was measured as return on assets (ROA) and return on investment (ROI) averaged over the 5-year period 1996-2000. The performance ratios were subsequently standardized within each of the two-digit SIC-code industries to eliminate industry effects from the data. The use of reported economic results was deemed appropriate since market returns could be skewed in the inflated market around the turn of the millennium. Financial leverage was measured as debt divided by equity averaged over the 5-year period 1996-2000 to control for spurious effects (Simerly and Li, 2000). Effective risk management was conceived as the extent to which the corporation is able to cope with environmental uncertainties and stabilize the earnings development. Hence, risk management was calculated as the standard deviation of corporate sales during 1996-2000 divided it by the standard deviation of economic performance during the same period to reach a direct indicator of the corporation's ability to dampen the influence of environmental risk factors.

Analyses

The hypotheses were tested in multiple regression analyses. One set of regressions used financial leverage as dependent variable and risk management as independent variable (O'Brien, 2003). Another set of regressions used the economic performance measures, i.e., 5-year average ROA and 5-year average ROI, as dependent variables and risk management as independent variable (Simerly and Li, 2000). The regressions considered a number of control variables. Organizational size may represent business diversification opportunities and organizational slack that could affect capital structure decisions (Aldrich, 1999; Aldrich and Auster, 1986), i.e., corporate size measured as the natural logarithm of total assets to correct for positive skew in the data was included in the regressions. A dummy variable was included to control for potential effects associated with agency and transaction cost issues (Kochar, 1998; Kochar and Hitt, 1998). The firm dummy indicates corporations with return on capital below −2.5 percent and capital growth below 25 percent and was assigned a value of 1 if the firm belonged to this subgroup where other firms were given a value of 0 (Simerli and Li, 2000). Firms belonging to these subgroups have not created returns in excess of the cost of capital during the period and, therefore, are likely to have agency or transaction cost problems that could affect capital structure decisions. The market-to-book ratio reflects the potential issue price of new equity in the firm, which might influence capital structure decisions (Hovakimian, Opler and Titman, 2001) and could predict market returns and performance (Fama and French, 1992, 1993). Financial leverage in itself may influence economic performance (Modigliani and Miller, 1958, 1963) and therefore was included as control variable in the performance regressions. Data sets causing error terms exceeding three times the standard deviation were analyzed and excluded from the regressions but their omission from the sample did not materially affect the results. Hence, the results reported here are based on the full sample. VIF factors calculated for all variables were within levels normally used to indicate potential multicollinearity problems (Kleinbaum, Kupper, Muller and Nizam, 1998; Lomax, 1992).

Results

Statistical data and correlation coefficients on the full sample are reported in Table 1.1 and the results from the subsequent regression analyses are shown in Table 1.2.

	1	2	3	4
1 5-yr ROA				
2 Leverage	-0.050[*]			
3 Size (ln assets)	0.147[**]	0.119[**]		
4 Market/Book	0.037	0.091[**]	0.402[**]	
5 Risk Management	0.269[**]	0.122[**]	0.764[**]	0.407[**]

N=1450; [+] $p < 0.10$; [*] $p < 0.05$; [**] $p < 0.01$

Table 1.1   Correlation Analysis

	Leverage	5-yr ROA	5-yr ROI
Leverage	-	-0.081[**]	-0.040
Performance	-0.087[**]	-	-
Size (ln assets)	0.044	0.104[**]	0.038
Firm Dummy	-0.044[+]	-0.041	-0.028
Market/Book	-0.042	0.061[*]	0.015
Risk Management	0.091[*]	0.386[**]	0.294[**]
Multiple R^2	0.027	0.095	0.072
Adjusted R^2	0.023	0.091	0.068
F-Significance	0.000	0.000	0.000

N=1450; [+] $p < 0.10$; [*] $p < 0.05$; [**] $p < 0.01$

Table 1.2   Regression Analyses (Standardized Regression Coefficients)

19

Discussion

The results from the regression analyses support the hypotheses and thereby give credence to the underlying arguments that effective risk management capabilities are associated with higher financial leverage and superior economic performance. Increasing competition among firms operating in global markets has accentuated the emphasis on corporate risk management practices (e.g., Froot, Scharfstein and Stein, 1993; Miller, 1998; Rawls and Smithson, 1990) and the exponential increase in the use of derivative instruments is testament to this development. However, longer term economic exposures and competitive risk factors cannot be hedged through the use of financial derivatives alone (Eiteman, Stonehill and Muffett, 1994), which is one reason for the emphasis on alternative risk-transfer instruments and the considerations of structural flexibilities and strategic responsiveness (e.g., Bettis and Hitt, 1995; Culp, 2002; Rangan, 1998). The increased use of derivatives and the recognition of operational flexibilities and strategic opportunities reflect attention to strategic risk management issues comprised within a more comprehensive enterprise risk management perspective (e.g., Lam, 2003; Miller, 1998). Hence, the proliferation of financial derivatives, insurance contracts, alternative risk-transfer instruments, and responsive strategic management processes should enhance the corporation's ability to withstand environmental uncertainty and exogenous shocks beyond management control (Froot, Sharfstein and Stein, 1993, 1994; Miller, 1998).

The findings are consistent with other studies of corporate risk management processes. For example, Liebenberg and Hoyt (2003) found that firms with higher financial leverage are more likely to appoint a Chief Risk Officer, i.e., there seems to be a common association between corporate emphasis on risk management and higher financial leverage as also found in this study. However, financial leverage in itself has a negative association with performance. Therefore, the results from this study seem to confirm that corporate risk management has a significant direct influence on the economic effects of capital structure choices. The fact that effective risk management seems to matter in corporate capital structure decisions can be partially explained by the dramatic increase in the use of derivatives and alternative risk-transfer instruments as well as an increased focus on enterprise risk management practices.

Conclusions

This study has presented an empirical analysis of a large cross sectional sample of corporations operating in different industries and demonstrated that effective risk management capabilities have a positive relationship to economic performance and are associated with higher financial leverage.

References

Aldrich H. E. (1999). *Organizations Evolving*. Newbury Park, CA, Sage.

Aldrich H. E. and Auster E. (1986). Even dwarfs started small: Liabilities of age and size and their strategic implications, in Staw B, Cummings, LL (eds.). *Research in Organizational Behavior, VIII*. JAI Press, Greenwich, CT.

Allen L. and Pantzalis C. (1996). Valuation of the operating flexibility of multinational corporations. *Journal of International Business Studies,* 27, 633-653.

Balakrisnan S. and Fox I. (1993). Asset specificity, firm heterogeneity and capital structure. *Strategic Management Journal,* 14, 3-16.

Barney J. B. (1991). Firm resources and sustained competitive advantage. *Journal of Management,* 17, 99-120.

Bettis R.A. and M. A. Hitt (1995). The new competitive landscape, *Strategic Management Journal,* 16, Special Issue, 7-19.

Chung K. H. (1993). Asset characteristics and corporate debt policy: An empirical test. *Journal of Business Finance,* 20, 83-98.

Culp C. L. (2002). *The ART of Risk Management: Alternative Risk Transfer, Capital Structure, and the Convergence of Insurance and Capital Markets*. Wiley, New York.

D'Aveni R. (1994). *Hypercompetition*. Free Press, New York.

DeLoach J. W. (2000). *Enterprise-Wide Risk Management*. Financial Times Prentice Hall, London.

Eiteman D. K., Stonehill A. I. and Moffett M. H. (1994). *Multinational Business Finance*. Addison-Wesley, Reading.

Fama E. F. and French K. R. (1992). The cross-section of expected stock returns. *Journal of Finance,* 47, 427-465.

Fama E. F. and French K. R. (1993). Common risk factors in returns on stocks and bonds. *Journal of Financial Economics,* 33, 3-56.

Froot K. A., Scharfstein D. S. and Stein J. C. (1993). Risk management: coordinating corporate investment and financing policies. *Journal of Finance,* 48 1629-1658.

Froot K. A., Scharfstein D. S. and Stein J. C. (1994). A framework for risk management. *Harvard Business Review,* 72(6), 91-102.

Froot K. A. (1999). The market for Catastrophe risk: a clinical examination. *The National Bureau of Economic Research.*

Harris M. and Raviv A. (1991). The theory of capital structure. *Journal of Finance,* 46, 297-355.

Hovakimian A., Opler T. and Titman S. (2001). The debt-equity choice. *Journal of Financial and Quantitative Analysis,* 36, 1-24.

Kleinbaum D.G., Kupper L.K., Muller K.E. and Nizam A. (1998). *Applied Regression Analysis and Other Multivariate Methods*, Third Edition. Duxbury Press, Pacific Grove, CA.

Kochar R. (1996). Explaining firm capital structure: The role of agency theory vs. transaction cost economics. *Strategic Management Journal,* 17, 713-728.

Kochar R. and Hitt M. A. (1998). Linking corporate strategy to capital structure: diversification strategy, type and source of financing. *Strategic Management Journal,* 19, 601-610.

Kogut B. and Kulatilaka N. (1994). Operating flexibility, global manufacturing and the option value of a multinational network. *Management Science,* 40, 123-138.

Lam J. (2003). *Enterprise Risk Management.* Wiley, Hoboken, NJ.

Liebenberg A. P. and Hoyt R. E. (2003). The determinants of enterprise risk management: evidence from the appointment of chief risk officers. *Risk Management and Insurance Review,* 6, 37-52.

Lomax R. G. (1992). *Statistical Concepts: A Second Course for Education and the Behavioral Sciences.* Longman, New York.

Merton R. C. (1995). Financial innovation and the management and regulation of financial institutions. *Journal of Banking & Finance,* 19, 461-481.

Miller K. D. (1998). Economic exposure and integrated risk management. *Strategic Management Journal,* 19, 497-514.

Modigliani F. and Miller M. H. (1958). The cost of capital, corporate finance and the theory of investment. *American Economic Review,* 48, 261-297.

Modigliani F. and Miller M. H.(1963). Corporate income taxes and the cost of capital: a correction. *American Economic Review,* 53, 433-443.

Myers S. C. (1984). The capital structure puzzle. *Journal of Finance,* 39, 575-592.

Myers S. C. and Majluf N. S. (1984). Corporate financing and investment decisions when firms have information that investors do not have. *Journal of Financial Economics,* 13, 187-221.

O'Brien J. P. (2003). The capital structure implications of pursuing a strategy of innovation. *Strategic Management Journal,* 24, 415-432.

Rangan S. (1998). Do multinationals operate flexibly? Theory and evidence. *Journal of International Business Studies,* 29, 217-237.

Rawls S. W. and Smithson C. W. (1990). Strategic risk management. *Journal of Applied Corporate Finance,* 2(2), 6-18.

Shimpi P. A. (1999). Integrating risk management and capital management, in Shimpi PA. (Ed.) *Integrating Corporate Risk Management.* Swiss Re New Markets, New York.

Simerly R. L. and Li M. (2000). Environmental dynamism, capital structure and performance: a theoretical integration and an empirical test. *Strategic Management Journal,* 21, 31-50.

Stulz R. (1990). Managerial discretion and optimal financing policies. *Journal of Financial Economics,* 26, 3-27.

Thies C. F. and Klock M. S. (1992). Determinants of capital structure. *Review of Financial Economics,* 1, 40-52.

Ward K. (1993). *Corporate Financial Strategy.* Butterworth Heinemann, Oxford, UK.

Williamson O. (1988). Corporate finance and corporate governance. *Journal of Finance,* 43, 567-591.

Williamson O. (1991). Comparative economic organization: the analysis of discrete structural alternatives. *Strategic Management Journal,* 36, 269-29.

CHAPTER 2

Risk Management

Karsten Andersen and Anette Terp

Editorial Comment

The insurance industry has considerable experience in assessing different types of risk and constitutes a substantive data reservoir on major risk events throughout the world. As a consequence, some of the larger insurance companies are well endowed to measure different risks and analyze them on an integrated basis and offer this as a service in addition to the general portfolio of insurance products. This article is a prime example of a comprehensive risk management program offered by a leading international insurance group. The descriptive data on the risk management environment presented in the article is based on proprietary information developed by Aon's internal research units[2].

Introduction

Risk taking is essential for any organization. Organizations need to understand the nature of the risks they encounter and prepare to manage them appropriately. Evaluating significance by estimating potential severity and likelihood of events is often not an exact science, and sometimes based on "best guesses" and "gut feelings". However, monitoring and managing significant exposures is essential in our world of today as many factors in our environment are changing with extreme speed.

No organization is isolated from its environment and a key aspect of managing risk will always be to manage the interface between strategic and operational activities and predicting the effect when the markets and even broader cultural, financial, political, and technological frameworks.

Developing Focus

The concept of risk is also changing, i.e., the society is showing an increasing tendency to unambiguously place responsibility when

---

[2] Risk Management and Risk Financing Survey, Aon Risk Consultants.

projected results differ from what was planned or when outcomes go off track. Earlier many companies perceived a large fire and the ensuing consequential business interruption loss as the worst damage that could occur but today organizations regard exposures such as product liability, damage to image or environmental damage equally important. In addition, today organizations are much more dependent on advanced technology, timely deliveries from vendors and subcontractors and on employees as one of the most important resources.

Risk - historic ranking	1995	1997	1999	2001	2004
Business Interruption	4	2	1	3	1
Employee Risk	3	3	6	10	2
General Liability			5	6	3
Failure to change				2	4
Fire / Physical damage	1	1	2	7	5
Loss of reputation			4	1	6
Professional liability	9	10	7		7
Product Liability	5	6	3	4	8
Directors and Officers liability		9		9	9
Recruitment				8	10

Figure 2.1   The Views of Risk Managers and CFO's 1995-2004

In an attempt to track the main trends in risk management and insurance, Aon has carried out bi-annual surveys for a number of years. The surveys reflect the views of risk and insurance managers and CFO's in a number of the world's largest companies. Figure 2.1 depicts the development of the top 10 risks over the period 1995 to 2004. From the survey results it can clearly be seen how the focus has changed.

Ten years ago, the top risks where all "insurable risks". While a number of these remain important, a number of other exposures, such as, "failure to change", "loss of reputation", and "recruitment difficulties" have entered the list of major concerns. However, we also notice that the list of perceived top exposures does not coincide 100% with the risk areas formally reviewed by the large companies as appears from Figure 2.2 below.

Risk Areas Formally Reviewed

Has your organization undertaken a formal analysis of any of the following areas?

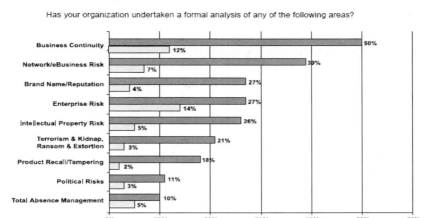

Figure 2.2   Risk Areas Formally Reviewed by Large Companies

Some of the expectations as to how listed companies in Denmark approach risk management are outlined in the Danish Corporate Governance recommendations, which states that:

Efficient risk management is a prerequisite for the board being able to perform the tasks for which it is responsible in the best possible way. Thus it is important that the board ensures that there are appropriate systems for risk management in place and, moreover, ensures that such systems meet the requirements of the company at any time.

Basically, the recommendations imply that

- Risks should be systematically identified
- Effective risk management systems should be put in place
- There should be continuous reporting on risk management activities

A review of annual reports from large listed companies in Denmark indicates that there is an increased focus on reporting the companies risk environments. In the late 1990's, most companies restricted themselves to mention currency risks, interest risks, credit risks, and Y2K risks. A few mentioned exposure to physical assets and intellectual properties. By 2004 the list had grown significantly and included risk areas such as:

- Business Ethics
- Changes in legislation
- Competitor actions
- Compliance with local legislation
- Contracts
- Currency
- Customer concentration
- Customer dependency
- Customers wants
- Divestments
- Recruitment and retention of employees and management
- Environment
- External factors
- Financial market risk
- Forward looking statements
- Health & Safety
- Interest rate
- Intellectual property
- IT dependency
- Legal risks
- Liquidity risks
- Market risks
- Mergers & Acquisitions
- Physical assets
- Product development
- Product safety
- Supplier dependency
- Tax
- Etc.

Whereas these areas are described in fairly generic terms, they do indicate that the companies are working more systematically and consciously with their risk environments.

Definition of Risk and Risk Management

Risk has been defined as internal and external uncertainties, events, or circumstances that the company must understand and manage effectively as it executes its strategies to achieve business objectives and create shareholder value. Basically, risk management can be defined as the process of doing this, meaning that the process should seek to eliminate, reduce, and control pure risks, enhance benefits, and avoid detriments from speculative exposures.

A distinction can be made between "pure risks" characterized by not having and "upside potential", i.e., no chance of gain. Many pure risks are also insurable, such as fire, health, and safety, environment, and security. In contrast, speculative risks (or business risks) are characterized by having an upside potential for gain as well as a downside risk of loss, such as interest rates, foreign exchange rates, research and development risks, etc.

Objectives of Risk Management

Organizations come in many shapes and sizes and vary significantly in the level of sophistication and degree of centralization. The specific objectives of risk management, therefore, naturally differ from organization to organization and depend on the specific risk environment of the company. Some of the more general objectives for risk management include:

Create Transparency

- ❏ Ensure that top management, the board of directors, the owners, and potential investors can evaluate the organization's significant exposures and appraise how they are dealt with by the organization.

Enhance Risk Awareness

- ❏ Create an organizational culture where risk awareness is an integral part of all management decisions and thus are taken into account when deciding on future business venues and where all employees can effectively handle the exposures that apply to their specific areas.

Control Risk Environment

- ❏ Minimize the probability - and potential severity - of future losses
- ❏ Ensure adequate financial protection against adverse events

- ❏ Establish and maintain preparedness to deal effectively with significant adverse events
- ❏ Minimize the overall "total cost of risk"

Focus on Risk Appetite
- ❏ Maximize the probability of success and minimize the risk of failure in reaching organizational objectives

Perspectives from the Insurance World

Risk Managers

From the perspective of today's insurance world, a risk manager is the person in charge of a corporation's insurance program and the person responsible for coordinating efforts to mitigate and monitor the safety and security issues that relate to insurable risks. Insurable risks, as mentioned, constitute pure risks, such as safety, fire, major hazards, security lapses, environmental hazards, etc.

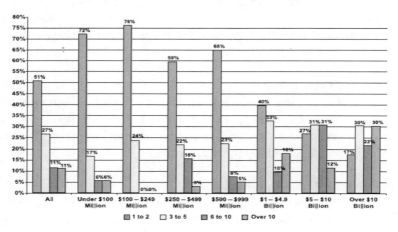

Risk Management Department Size

How many staff members are there in the risk management department?

Figure 2.3   Number of Employees in Risk Management Departments

Normally, risk management departments are organized as staff functions reporting through the financial or legal departments, are relatively lean, and staffed with specialists. Risk managers have, therefore, always relied on the support of and input from internal and external resources to manage the organization's "insurable" risk environment. Most risk management departments only have a few people employed and only among the largest corporations do we see departments with more than 10 employees (Figure 2.3).

Risk managers, as defined above, are not involved in managing all the different risks that may expose the corporation. Different types of risk are often handled in specialized functional areas (Figure 2.4).

Identify the departments with whom risk management works closely.

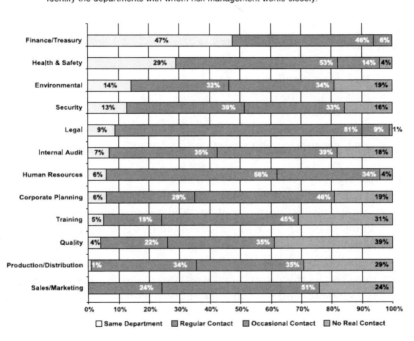

Figure 2.4   Distribution of Risk Management Responsibilities

Hence, financial risk management is typically handled by a Treasury Department, legal exposures are handled by a Legal Department, R&D exposures are the concern of the R&D Department, etc. Ultimately, the overall responsibility for all the risks in the corporation rests with the CEO and the Board of Directors.

From an insurance perspective, risk management relates to managing the pure risks discussed earlier, and the concept "total cost of risk", relates to the insurance premiums, retained losses, cost of risk management, administration, and education/training incurred to handle these risks. With effective risk management and the appropriate financing of the insurable risks it is possible to reduce "total cost of risk" and release resources that can be used to pursue other organizational goals. Thereby, effective risk management can become a parameter for competitive advantage just like the development of markets and products.

Risk Management

Risk Management can be seen as a continuous management process where significant exposures are systematically identified, evaluated, and managed. Normally, the process is described as a five-step progression:

- Risk identification
- Risk evaluation
- Risk control
- Risk financing
- Risk monitoring and reporting

Risk Identification

During the identification phase relevant exposures are identified. Several more or less formalized methods are available and used in combination to obtain a broad picture of the risk environment. The first is normally looking at what the organization does, i.e., how it achieves its overall objectives and considers what events can prevent it from doing this. This is often combined with looking at the past experiences of the organization and business community with an attempt to project what new exposures will arise in the future from changing legislation, activities, markets, etc.

Some exposures have the potential to be "life-threatening" for the company but are highly unlikely to occur, other events occur very frequently, but have relatively small adverse consequences. In order to deal with an exposure, it needs to be identified, and risk identification can therefore be seen as the most important step in the risk management process.

• **Analyze operations**	Information about the company's operations in the past, present and future is an important source to give a first rough impression of the significant exposures.
• **Review production flowcharts**	Insight to how value is created is equally important: Where are the production bottlenecks, key machinery, processes and equipment? What is the current protection level and what options are available for redirecting production flow?
• **Evaluate contracts and documents**	Review of contracts and documents can give an evaluation of the amount of "off-balance" assets and liabilities. Brand, rights and Intellectual property owned is an important means of identifying exposures. How is contractual obligations, liability and guarantees reviewed, evaluated and controlled?
• **Review financial records and financial statements**	The financial statements will normally indicate the level of financial exposures (currency, credit, interest risks etc.). How are these exposures monitored, controlled and reported?
• **Conduct interviews with internal and external experts**	Key persons/experts within the company normally have very precise ideas of the significant exposures, but often these are not reported or evaluated in a common format. Internal experts are aware of most "near-misses" and thus have valuable information in what can go wrong.
	External experts can contribute with tools, systematic approach and experience from other companies with similar exposures.
	Developing and using questionnaires and generic risk registers is a means of systemising and ensuring consistency in the process. No questionnaire or register can be expected to be exhaustive list of the potential exposures, but can be used as inspiration.
• **Analyse records of historic losses**	Recording and analysing what has occurred in the past often gives a good indication of what could happen in the future.
	As disastrous losses are very rare, own records are not always adequate and it is a good idea also to review and analyse what has happened for others with comparable exposures.

Table 2.1   Important Source of Risk in Risk Identification Analysis

A number of generic techniques can be used to identify exposures. The following tabulates some important sources for use in the risk identification process (Table 2.1).

To keep things in appropriate proportions it makes sense to focus on the most significant corporate risk factors for further work. It is, therefore, not advisable to engage in a labour intensive endeavour to identify all possible exposures of the company.

Risk Evaluation

Obviously, not all exposures are equally important to the organization. Hence exposures should be prioritized to focus mitigating efforts on the most significant ones. A normal approach for prioritizing risks is reviewing the potential severity of the exposures and their probability of occurrence. The product of these two dimensions is a measure of the expected costs of the risk exposure and the highest of these should be given due attention.

Risk evaluation can be both very simple and very complex. The "simple" best guess or gut-feel of top management or in-house experts should not be underestimated and the more "complex" and analytic stochastic modeling should not be overestimated. The important thing is to choose the level of sophistication that makes the most sense in specific situations and that will provide an adequate foundation for decision-making.

Many risk assessment tools/models have been developed to assist in the process, e.g., ALARP, Fault Tree Analysis, AS/NZS 4360: 1999, etc., some of which analyze specific risks. In recent years a variety of IT supported risk management/assessment tools have been developed in the insurance industry to provide their customers with appropriate tools to evaluate pure risks.

The risk assessment process requires management commitment and the necessary time and resources to be available. One or more risk assessment techniques may be used at the same time depending on the specific conditions of the individual enterprise, but a risk assessment work plan should undoubtedly utilize a rigorous methodology to analyze risks in the process of providing qualitative and a quantitative risk assessments.

Before starting the risk assessment process it is essential to consider a proper methodology that can be adopted by the organization in question. It is however important to have in mind that no matter what methodology is used both the data forming the basis for the analysis, the analysis process itself, and the recommendations that eventually are the outcome of the process, will all be based on human judgments whether made by specialists or non-specialists. When the risk assessment is based on judgment it becomes even more important to have ongoing risk monitoring and if necessary a repeating risk assessment process. The latter is of course particularly relevant to companies operating in rapidly changing industries and competitive business environments.

The process of mapping the identified scenarios based on the estimated frequencies and severities allows a ranking and selection of the most significant risks for further treatment. Besides intuitive evaluation of importance, the selection criteria should consider:

- Scenarios with highest estimated annual impact
- Scenarios with potential to threaten survival of the company
- Scenarios that require minimal resources to fix

For each of the scenarios selected for further evaluation and analysis, a plan of action must be specified. The action plan must contain specific objectives and should as a minimum clarify:

- Who "owns the risk" and coordinates the efforts?
- What further analysis and mitigating efforts need to be initiated?
- What is the time schedule?
- What should the outcome be?
- Who follows up on progress?

Risk Control

Conceptually, five strategies are available to control an exposure. The five strategies are:

- Avoidance
- Prevention
- Reduction
- Segregation
- Transfer

Avoidance focuses on eliminating the risk completely. Prevention is focused on reducing the probability of occurrence. Reduction tries to reduce the severity associated with events. Segregation focuses on the division of exposed entities to achieve risk diversification and reduce the aggregate affect from events. Transfer relates to the transfer of the ultimate liability (not just the financial burden) to (an)other organization(s). The five generic risk control strategies are almost always used in combination. There are distinct benefits to this approach as it ensures a comprehensive and systematic review of the overall exposure and the spectrum of possible solutions.

Avoidance
Avoidance will be a decision not to create a particular loss exposure or to completely eliminate an existing exposure. Such a decision will reduce the probability of a given loss to zero, but it has very limited application. For example, avoiding risk – both pure and strategic risks – associated with being in a particular industry or occupation requires never entering, or immediately leaving, that industry or occupation. Suppose that for some reason an organization wants to avoid the risk of being in the tobacco business. First, this would mean that the organization would have to completely stay away from manufacturing, buying, or selling any products or services that relate to the tobacco industry. Secondly, on a more sophisticated level, avoiding the risk would mean that the organization would have to refrain from buying or selling anything from or to other organizations that one way or another are involved in the tobacco industry (Figure 2.5).

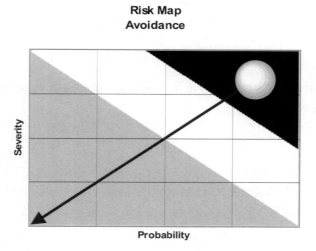

Figure 2.5 Assessing the Risk Avoidance Strategy

Given the complex interdependencies among organizations avoidance is often a very difficult risk control strategy, so other strategies has to be taken into consideration when managing risks.

Prevention

Risk prevention is any measure that reduces the probability of a loss occurring. The risk is not completely eliminated, but with effective prevention measures the risk can be minimized to an acceptable level of probability/frequency (Figure 2.6).

Risk Map
Prevention

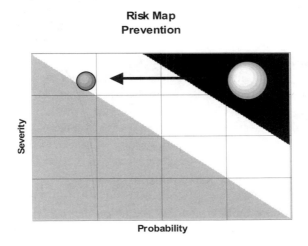

Figure 2.6   Assessing the Risk Prevention Strategy

Most risk prevention measures are related to how losses are caused. In general, a risk prevention measure is concerned with creating operational procedures or installing physical safeguards before the risk turns into a loss in order to break the chain of circumstances or causes that are thought to lead to the loss. Breaking the chain could either stop the loss from happening or at least reduce the probability that it will occur.

An example of prevention: Fire safety engineers speak of the "fire triangle" – the three elements of fuel, oxygen and ignition source that must be present for a fire to occur. Removing one of the three elements will prevent the fire from occurring.

Reduction

Risk Reduction is different from risk prevention because reduction focuses on reducing the severity of a loss that eventually will occur (Figure 2.7).

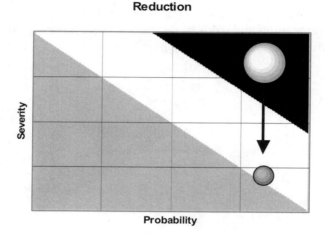

Risk Map
Reduction

Figure 2.7   Assessing the Risk Reduction Strategy

To analyze opportunities of risk reduction a risk manager must imagine that a loss has occurred and then analyze what could have been done, either before or after the loss occurred in order to reduce the severity (size/extent).

Risk reduction is a valid risk management strategy for both pure and strategic risks. An example of risk reduction measure for pure risks is erecting a firewall, installing fire suppression system, etc. Reducing business losses (strategic risk) normally involves either reducing an organization's commitment to a particularly risky venture, creating "limited" companies, avoiding "mother company guarantees, etc.

Segregation

This risk management strategy encompasses two different but closely related risk management techniques – separation or duplication of the exposed units. The purpose of both is to reduce an organization's dependency on any single asset, activity or person and at the same time make individual risks smaller and more predictable. The proverb "Don't put all your eggs in one basket" is another way of describing segregation.

Separation means dividing assets or operation into two or more separate units and in the pure risk area an example could be dividing stock into two warehouses instead of one. Duplication is as the word says, a complete reproduction of an organization's own standby asset or facility to keep in reserve (Figure 2.8). The duplication will only be used if and when the primary asset or facility is damaged. Examples of pure risk duplication are ensuring back up of computer files and keeping spare parts for key machinery in stock can be mentioned.

Risk Map
Segregation

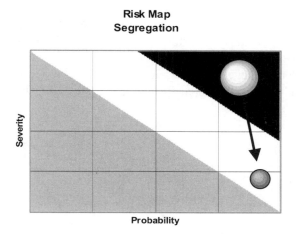

Figure 2.8 Assessing the Risk Segregation Strategy

Transfer
Transfer is the process of shifting the ultimate responsibility of an exposure to another legal entity outside the company, e.g., by using subcontractors, or outsourcing to independent vendors who are better equipped to handle the exposure in a professional manner.

Depending on the nature of the transfer and of how well the independent vendor is able to control the risk, there may still be a residual exposure with a potential to cause a loss for the company. Hence, if a company outsources all its transportation needs to an independent supplier it has eliminated the direct transportation exposures. However, it may thereby have created a level of dependency on the supplier. For example, if the supplier is not able to meet the requirements for quality and timeliness, it will reflect poorly on company image.

Risk Financing

As risks are rarely totally eliminated some means of financial protection are required. The default instrument is withdrawing from current revenues or activating the balance sheet. That is, if no other measure is implemented, the organization has to register a current expense directly on the balance sheet. In the case of pure risks, insurance protection is the predominant tool to obtain financial protection. For financial risks, various financial instruments are available to hedge the exposures. The shareholders will finance the vast majority of other operational and strategic risks directly.

Risk financing almost always constitutes a combination between retaining and transferring different portions of the potential costs of losses. In order to achieve the objective of minimizing total cost of risk, the retention level must be selected according to market pricing of the transfer tool as illustrated in the very basic figure below (Figure 2.9).

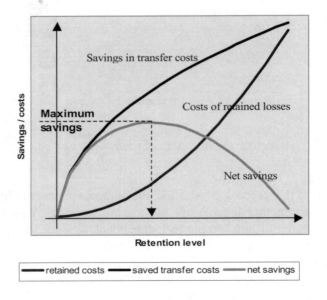

Figure 2.9   The trade-off Between Risk Transfer and Retention

The top curve illustrates the savings in transfer costs when higher deductibles are accepted. The lower curve illustrates the retained costs of accepting higher retention levels. The middle curve is the difference between the two and represents the net savings. At the maximum level of this curve, the savings are the largest and indicate the optimal deductible level.

In the insurance world there is no exact formula for the discount of a higher deductible level, so it will have to be tested through marketing exercises at regular intervals. The expected costs of accepting a higher retention level can be calculated from simulations of historic losses, but this requires detailed knowledge of these (i.e. systematic recording and reporting of losses).

Retention can be organized in a number of ways. In general, the larger the organization, the more sophisticated methods are used. As depicted in the table below (Table 2.2), the larger the organization the more captives are used for insurance purposes. Basically a captive is an insurance company that is typically used only by the owner of the company.

Revenue: Retention Methods	All	Under $100M	$100 – $249M	$250 – $499M	$500 – $999M	$1 – $4.9B	$5 – $10B	Over $10B
Corporate Level Deductibles/Retentions	78%	66%	77%	72%	85%	92%	79%	92%
Local Deductibles/Retentions	32%	19%	25%	33%	24%	40%	50%	63%
Captive Insurance Company	19%	8%	6%	5%	4%	36%	39%	54%
Cell in a Protected Cell Company (PCC)	1%	0%	0%	2%	0%	1%	0%	0%
Rent-a-Captive	1%	0%	0%	0%	0%	2%	0%	4%

Table 2.2   The Relationship Between Company Size and Retention

In order to ensure adequate funding in case of a major loss, a worst-case scenario is normally estimated in financial terms. Such an estimate is determined from a series of technical calculations, which are based on internationally agreed assumptions. An estimated property loss in the area measured in hundreds of millions and an estimated business interruption loss measured in the low billions over a couple of years is not unusual for key production facilities at larger corporations. The insurance program is designed to cope with such a loss but is very rarely used to the full extent.

It is remarkable that the very same corporations can suffer a much greater loss in the volatile stock market due to poorly handled media relations without taking much notice. Part of the explanation is bound to be that the latter is normally not life threatening and unless a new stock issue is imminent, the share price will not have a direct impact on the company's cash flow. However, if the stock is traded on the day, the owners may lose much more on "normal hiccups in the market" than on a dreaded worst-case scenario loss.

As the required high capacities on the various insurance lines are rarely used, there has been focus on bundling the exposures and financing them together and thereby utilizing portfolio diversification effects between the exposures, eliminating over-protection.

What risk management and risk financing technique to use will depend on the appetite of the individual organization in this area, the overall goal of the organization, and the organization's level of ambition with respect to risk management and retention, etc.

In the insurance industry this is done when bundling insurable risks in so-called multi-line insurance programs. The available capacity for multi-line programs can be somewhat limited and, therefore, will not always offer competitive financing terms compared to more traditional insurance products.

Risk Monitoring/Reporting

The last, or the first step, in the cyclical risk management process is to monitor performance and adjust controls, preparedness, and financing arrangements accordingly. The ever-changing environment comprising changes in legislative, market, and competitive conditions require continuous evaluation and adjustment of the mitigating controls and risk exposure measures. Besides adjustment, an important objective of this phase is to keep the management and shareholders of the company abreast with the significance of the exposures, how they are controlled, and how the organization is prepared to deal with adverse events.

It is, therefore, necessary to stay informed about how the organizational system is currently working and how new environmental developments may affect the risk exposures. This needs to be done both locally by business segment, by geographical region globally and nationally, and also centrally at the corporate group level.

At the corporate level this can be accomplished through frequent risk management reporting, which is consolidated and analysed on the national, regional, and corporate levels. This also provides a basis to design and adjust global insurance programs.

Conclusion

Managing risks has always been an integral part of the managerial responsibility in the company. However, factors such as increased specialization, market concentration, globalization, and larger interdependency between companies have undoubtedly changed the level of what is acceptable risk and what is not. In addition to this, today's media coverage leaves very little room to "learn as you go" in case of a crisis. This has forced many companies towards a more explicit and systematic approach in handling their risk environment.

With effectively controlled risk exposures the potential loss impact is reduced but not eliminated. While losses will eventually happen a systematic assessment of the risk environment can ensure preparedness and adequate financial protection to cope with adverse events. Another potential benefit is that better control of the risk environment can allow the company to engage in operations that otherwise would be considered too risky and therefore avoided.

The all-embracing motive for managing risks in many enterprises is that a controlled risk environment will prevent "surprises" from arising and minimize the total costs of risks, which can release economic funds for other value enhancing purposes.

CHAPTER 3

The Risk-Return Effects of Strategic Responsiveness: A Simulation Analysis[3]

Torben Juul Andersen and Richard A. Bettis

Strategic responsiveness is considered an important determinant of an organization's value creation potential in dynamic knowledge-based markets. Hence, this article presents a simulation model that explores how market learning, knowledge adjustment, and strategic repositioning affect the risk-return relationships in uncertain market environments.

Introduction

A new knowledge-based economic order characterized by on-going innovation and rapidly changing market conditions seems to be emerging (D'Avenie, 1994; Grant, 1996). In this hypercompetitive environment superior performance arguably depends on corporate capabilities that enhance the ability to learn about the current market environment and thereby allow the corporation to consider adapting its strategic position in response to changing market conditions (Bettis and Hitt, 1995; Teece, Pisano and Shuen, 1997; Eisenhardt and Martin, 2000). Accordingly, this article adopts organizational learning, knowledge creation, and strategic responsiveness perspectives to develop a model that simulates the performance effects of new market insights and corporate repositioning.

Whereas sustainable competitive advantage is assumed to rest on existing firm-specific competencies (Barney, 1986), the focus on dynamic capabilities suggests that ongoing value creation is associated with learning processes that enhance the corporation's ability to be strategically responsive (Lei, Hitt and Bettis, 1996; Teece, Pisano and

---

[3] Parts of this article are based on Andersen, T. J. and Bettis, R. A. (2002). Analyzing the performance effects of strategic response capabilities. Paper presented at the Academy of Management Annual Conference, Denver, CO, USA.

Shuen, 1997). However, these contentions have not been systematically investigated vis-à-vis the corporate value creation potential in dynamic markets. As argued by Ilinitch, D'Aveni and Lewin (1996): "further research is needed on...how....to manage organizations that can respond to the uncertainties...of hypercompetitive environments". Hence, a key motivation of this study is to investigate the value creation effects of learning as a knowledge adjusting process that provide the organization with market insights that allow it to change strategic position in the face of changing market conditions. The model investigates the effects of learning ands adjustment of market knowledge that provide the basis for alternative strategic responses and eventual corporate decisions to change market position. Uncertainty is incorporated as ongoing stochastic changes in market conditions as reflective of hypercompetition while periodic cash generation and the volatility of the cash flows constitute central outcome variables.

Organizational Learning and Strategic Response Capabilities

Organizational learning has been conceived in a number of ways. A predominant perspective describes learning as action improvement from changes in organizational behavior induced by perceived performance shortfalls and more complete knowledge (Argyris and Schön, 1978; Fiol and Lyles, 1985). Under-performance is ascribed to misperceptions, miscommunication, and the inertia of organizational routines and, therefore, learning takes place when organizational members confront these 'espoused theories' with their 'theories-in-use' (Argyris, 1982) or 'mental models' (Senge, 1990). That is, when individual perceptions are confronted with reality and the managers' beliefs are aligned with reality, then the organization learns. This view implies that managerial perceptions can be uncovered and adjusted through learning processes to capture an underlying true setting. However, the firm's creative behavior and constructive responsiveness to a changing market environment may be just as important (Alveson, 1993). Nonaka and Takeuchi (1995) describe such a knowledge creation process assuming a distinct view of knowledge "... as a dynamic human process" (Nonaka, 1994). This conceptualization of learning is consistent with hypercompetition where ongoing innovation constantly changes the competitive environment (D'Aveni, 1994; Thomas, 1996).

Organizational learning has been classified as process refinement and search to change existing routines (Levitt and March, 1988). These kinds of learning are variously referred to as 'learning I' and 'learning II' (Bateson, 1972), 'single' and 'double loop' learning (Argyris and Schön, 1978), and 'first' and 'second order' learning (Fiol and Lyles, 1985). In first order learning, existing competencies are made more efficient by perfecting current practices. Under first order learning existing competencies are improved by perfecting current practices. In contrast, second order learning creates new knowledge that allows the organizations to change practices. Singular adherence to particular distinctive competencies can become a 'trap' that withholds the organization from considering new responses to changing market conditions (Levinthal and March, 1991). That is, knowledge updating through learning is imperative to enable an organization to respond to market changes and probably should comprise elements of both 'first' and 'second order' learning to strike a reasonable balance between exploitation and exploration (March, 1991).

The organizational learning perspective is consistent with the concept of dynamic capabilities that reflect a corporate ability to modify existing and develop new competencies that create competitive advantage in turbulent environments (Lei, Hitt and Bettis, 1996; Teece, Pisano and Shuen, 1997). It is argued that competitive advantage arises from learning and knowledge creation that increase the range of possible corporate actions (Huber, 1991). The creation of potential actions resembles identification of 'latent' options that extend strategic choices available to management (Bowman and Hurry, 1993). The more the organization can consider alternative action, the higher the possibilities of changing market position in uncertain environments. These relationships are illustrated in Figure 3.1.

Constant search of external market conditions and openness to change are necessary conditions for strategic response capabilities (Bettis and Hitt, 1995; Teece, Pisano and Shuen, 1997). The ability to learn about environmental change is influenced by managers' cognitive understanding reflected in their belief structures (Kiesler and Sproull, 1982; Nyström and Starbuck, 1984). Hence, to learn and gain new insights organizations must be willing to discard parts of their existing environmental beliefs and managers unlearn when they are willing to change their 'dominant logic' (Prahalad and Bettis, 1986). Challenging prevailing beliefs facilitates knowledge adaptation and successful firms generally show an urge to change even when they are successful (Nonaka and Takeuchi, 1995; Leonard-Barton, 1995). Managers' mental models may also decay over time as organizational practices gradually are taken out of use (Klein, 1989). Invariably, learning will capture a combination of these types of knowledge creation, unlearning, and decay processes.

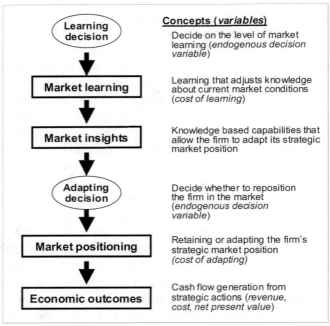

Figure 3.1   Market Learning and Market Positioning

Market learning describes a search process to acquire insights about current market conditions. The ability to establish better market insights is a knowledge creating capability and provides the firm with an alternative choice to adapt its strategic market position so it is more in tune with current market conditions. Market learning captures characteristics of both 'first' and 'second-order' learning. For example, the market may only require higher quality products that can be introduced at relatively low cost as incremental product adaptations on the basis of existing routines. Market learning may also find that customers want a significantly different set of product attributes than the firm is configured to deliver, i.e., if the firm decides to adapt its market position in this case, it will require a more costly reconfiguration of the firm's value chain that changes existing routines. Market learning allows a firm to see ways in which it can adapt its strategic market position in view of new insights about market conditions. This should be particularly beneficial to firms operating in highly uncertain market environments. To the extent that refined insights about market conditions can enhance the ability to respond, market learning should improve economic performance and reduce the volatility in periodic economic outcomes. These arguments are captured in the following hypotheses.

HYPOTHESIS 1: *Market learning has a positive association with corporate performance*

HYPOTHESIS 2: *Environmental uncertainty has a positive moderating effect on the performance relationship of market learning*

HYPOTHESIS 3: *Market learning has a negative association with ex post performance risk*

Market learning is a path dependent process as it adjusts existing knowledge about the market from one period to the next, and the positive performance effects from market learning emerge over time as corporate managers use new market insights and decide to change strategic market position to be better aligned with current market conditions (Kogut and Zander, 1992; Teece, Pisano and Shuen, 1997). Empirical studies of these phenomena require meticulous field observations over extended periods of time and such longitudinal studies represent tremendous practical barriers. In contrast, computerized model simulations provide a time efficient approach to study longitudinal processes that has been adopted in operations research, economics, and organizational studies (e.g., Cyert and March, 1992; Levy, 1994; Chatman and Barsade, 1995). Accordingly, a simulation model was developed here to analyze the effects of market learning on performance and performance risk over an extended number of time periods.

The Simulation Model

The model describes how a process of market learning, knowledge adjustment, and strategic positioning affects the organization's cash flow generation under uncertain market conditions. The level of uncertainty characterizes the external market environment where low uncertainty reflects conditions in stable industries and high uncertainty reflects conditions in dynamic industries. The organization can engage in learning about changing market conditions and new insights generated from this process allow management to decide whether the firm should adapt its strategic position to obtain a better match with prevailing market conditions. Hence, management can take discretionary actions in two ways under conditions of market uncertainty. That is, they can engage in learning about the market environment and they can decide whether or not to adapt the firm's position in accordance with the knowledge acquired from the learning process. These discretionary actions will affect economic performance because revenues are assumed to be larger when the actual firm position is close to the current market condition in each period while revenues are lower when there is a mismatch between firm position and market condition. Whereas market learning has potential advantages it is not without downsides because the firm will incur a cost related to engagement in the learning process and will face a restructuring cost when the firm's market position is adapted from one period to the next. Hence, the firm's economic performance is equal to the periodic net cash flows determined as periodic revenues minus the cost of learning and adapting in each period. The firm's value creation potential is determined by the net present value of the future cash flows and risk is calculated as the volatility of the periodic cash flows.

The model depicts market learning as a process by which the firm can obtain new market insights about current market conditions (Sinkula, Baker and Noordewier, 1997). Once new insights have been obtained, the firm is able to use that information to change market position in response to changing market conditions. The firm can engage in different levels of market learning, expressed by a learning rate, and the level of learning, in turn, determines the firm's ability to gain new insights and thereby its ability to change market position. Organizational perceptions and beliefs are not specified in the model as the management team is assumed to engage actively in the learning process.

A central variable in the model captures the market condition at time t indicated by a number (M_t). Initially, the market condition is set at a random number fixed between 0 and 1, which is then changed from period to period by adding a market uncertainty component (υ) to the previous period's market condition ($M_{t+1} = M_t + \upsilon$). Market uncertainty is modeled as a stochastic process represented by a randomly drawn number from a normal distribution with a mean of zero, so the market condition can vary in both positive and negative direction over time. This 'white noise' element describes environmental uncertainty and reflects continuous changes in market conditions caused by exogenous factors beyond management control.

The firm's market position can be adapted by using new market insights gained from the learning process to position the firm closer to prevailing conditions.

The firm can adhere to different levels of market learning expressed by a learning rate (λ) indicating the level of learning performed to get new market insights. Market learning requires organizational resources and, therefore, imposes a cost on the firm in every period proportional to the learning rate. In any given period, the firm can use new market insight gained from the learning process and move toward the current market condition by an amount equal to the difference between the market condition revealed through the learning process and the firm's actual market position multiplied by the learning rate ($\lambda(M_t - F_t)$). Hence, the more the firm is engaged in learning, the better the opportunities to change strategic market position. When the learning rate is set at 1 it means that management gets full insight about current market conditions, i.e., perfect learning. The learning rate is set at different values in the simulations (0, 0.1, 0.2, 0.3, 0.4, 0.5, 0.6, 0.7, 0.8, 0.9, 1.0, 1.1, and 1.2) and held constant throughout each simulation to analyze the effects of different emphasis on learning. The simulations allow the possibility that the managers overshoot their interpretation of market conditions in the learning process ($\lambda>1$). A learning rate above 1 reflects inefficient learning because the magnitude of the market's move is overestimated while paying a higher price for the learning process.

The firm is rewarded the closer its actual market position is to the current market condition in each period. So, the smaller the difference is between the firm's actual market position and the current market condition ($|M_t - F_t|$) the higher the revenues will accrue to the firm. In this model, the relationship is expressed as a simple linear revenue function ($R_t = a_0 + b_0|M_t - F_t|$). Market learning adjusts the firm's insights about the current market condition and thereby gives the firm an opportunity to change market position and the cost of changing market position is proportional to the size of the required change in the firm's market position. The firm can use the acquired market insights to change and update its market position in every period. The firm's net cash flow in each period (CF_t) is determined as the difference between revenues and the costs incurred from market learning and adaptation to the firm's market position and the firm's value creation potential is calculated as the net present value of the future cash flows. The risk is determined as the volatility (annualized standard deviation) of the firm's periodic cash flows. The general model of market learning is shown in Figure 3.2.

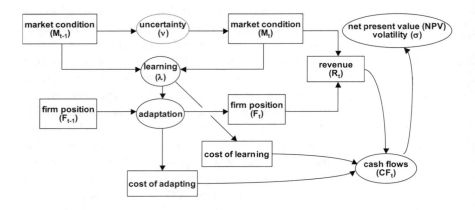

Figure 3.2   A General Model of Market Learning

The simulations were performed with five different levels of uncertainty ranging from low to high reflected by different standard deviations of the stochastic uncertainty function. The revenue function is sensitive to the market mismatch position ($R_t = 4000-900(|M_t - F_t|)$). The simulations were applied under thirteen different learning rates ranging from 0 to 1.2 (Table 3.1).

Results

Ten simulations were performed in each of the scenarios characterized by level of uncertainty and learning rate. In each of these runs, the firm's periodic cash flows were calculated over 80 consecutive periods ($t=80$). The simulations determined the cash flow generation, net present value of cash flows, and volatility of the cash flows. An initial increase in the learning rate from 0 to the 0.2-0.5 range is associated with higher value creation (net present values) but there are diminishing returns to learning. In environments with low uncertainty, the optimal learning rate is around 0.2. In environments with high uncertainty, the optimal learning rate is around 0.5 (Figure 3.3). The optimal learning rate is reached well before a rate of 1, which corresponds to perfect learning. Hence, market learning clearly has a positive effect on value creation and, therefore, supports hypothesis 1.

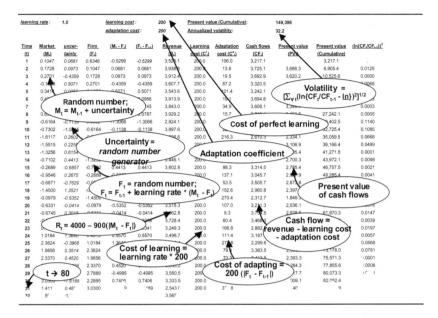

Table 3.1　Simulating the Market Learning Model – An Example

However, it does not pay to seek complete adjustment to market changes when there is environmental uncertainty.

There is a high value creation penalty when market learning is neglected (a learning rate of 0) and the penalty is considerably higher under uncertainty. Accordingly, the benefits from an increase in the learning rate from 0 to 0.2 and 0.3 are significantly larger under high uncertainty, which supports hypothesis 2. When the learning rate is increased from 0 to 0.1, 0.2, and 0.3, the volatility of periodic cash flow generation is reduced at all levels of uncertainty (Figure 3.4). This lends general support for hypothesis 3.

However, as the learning rate increases above 0.3, cash flow volatility starts to rise again. This phenomenon arises because the higher adaptation costs reduce the benefits derived from market positioning and makes economic performance more vulnerable. In general, the simulations show an inverse relationship between value creation and cash flow volatility across all scenarios (Figure 3.5).

The cost factors have comparable influences on performance as both higher costs of learning and adapting have negative effects on cash flows and value creation. Hence, the cost elements influence the optimal learning rate, i.e., the higher the cost of learning and adapting, the lower the optimal learning rate.

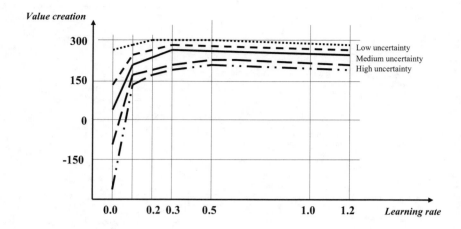

Figure 3.3   Simulation Results - Value Creation and Learning Rate

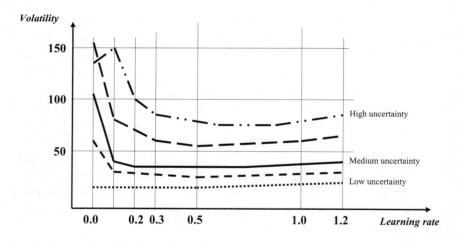

Figure 3.4   Simulation Results - Volatility and Learning Rate

Furthermore, the cost of adapting influences risk (volatility) in the model, as market learning associated with low adaptation costs reduces cash flow volatility. In other words, the better the firm is positioned to reconfigure, the higher the value creation effect of market learning. A firm can exploit favorable market insights achieved from market learning by enhancing the net present value of future cash flows and reducing the volatility of periodic cash flows.

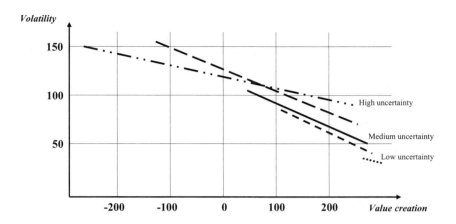

Figure 3.5   Simulation Results - Volatility and Value Creation

Discussion

The results provide evidence of a positive relationship between some market learning and value creation where the incremental value creation effect is particularly strong under high market uncertainty. Market learning allows the firm to observe new market developments and the acquired market insight provides the firm with the ability to adapt its market position and respond to current market conditions, i.e., the firm's strategic responsiveness is enhanced. The ability to restructure and change the firm's strategic market position to better reflect current market conditions generally improves the firm's revenue stream. Hence, complete neglect of market learning is clearly a disadvantage to firms operating in changing market environments. To extrapolate this phenomenon into real examples, *Nordstrom* was long the industry benchmark for premier customer service and customer relations, but also relied heavily on this competence after it stopped paying off. In other words, the company was not able to sense changes in its customers' needs and adapt its market offerings accordingly. In contrast, retailers like *Abercrombie & Fitch*, *Gap* and *Intimate Brands* were successful providers of high quality and moderately priced goods targeted to specific customer segments all the while they experimented with diverse sales channels, such as, retail chains, catalogues, and websites. We find similar examples in different industries. For example, *Silicon Graphics* saw a dramatic drop in sales because they lacked a more intimate sharing of their customers' needs. In contrast, other leaders in the server market, such as *Sun*

57

Microsystems and *Hewlett-Packard*, were doing quite well by adapting their products to specialized industry applications and focusing on emerging needs for support, education, and professional services to their customers.

Engaging in learning to gain new market insights can enable the firm to adapt under changing market conditions and thereby increase the value creation potential. Conversely, there is no guarantee that an absolute amount of market knowledge will enable the firm to create value under the uncertainty of future market conditions because it is constantly changing. Thus, value potential depends on the firm's engagement in ongoing market learning and knowledge adjustment that allow the firm to change and adapt its strategic market position. Consequently, economic performance may reverse quickly in turbulent environments if the firm's knowledge about the market is not adjusted and molded through market learning on a continuous basis

There seems to be a general sense that more learning is always better in hypercompetitive environments arguing that higher learning rates are needed when markets change more frequently (Stata, 1994). Whereas the simulation results indicate that the optimal learning rate is higher in dynamic compared to stable environments, they also show that there are significant limitations in the incremental value enhancement achieved from learning beyond a certain threshold level. Market learning can be a somewhat costly process and the firm may have to commit substantial resources to restructure and adapt the organization, so it is not obvious that more learning will always pays off. The analysis shows that some learning is good but the net benefits from higher levels of learning become increasingly doubtful. Value creation from learning in turbulent environments depends on the cost of learning and adapting. Hence, an organization that is able to learn at low costs will gain more advantage from learning. Similarly, an agile and flexible organization will reap greater benefits from market learning activities because the costs of restructuring are low.

The calculation of two outcome variables, the net present value and cash flow volatility, provide a basis for analyzing the risk-return relationship. The results underscore that market learning can enhance economic performance and at the same time reduce performance volatility particularly when market uncertainty is high. In other words, the firm displays a negative relationship between value creation and cash flow volatility when the firm adheres to a certain degree of market learning. This also means that in market environments where ex ante business risk is perceived to be high, engagement in market learning may lead to higher economic performance and lower performance volatility at the same time. This result is contrary to predictions derived from financial investment theory where higher returns are associated with higher risk (Sharpe, 1964; Lintner, 1965). However, the findings are consistent with Bowman's (1980, 1982) studies where he found inverse relationships between ROE and the standard deviation of returns across industries. As part of Bowman's explanation for this unexpected relationship, he asserted that good management may impose higher returns and lower business risk at the same time. The simulation results support these assertions and explain how inverse ex post risk return relationships can arise.

There are advantages associated with the use of a simple model in an exploratory study like this. The basic model provides insights about fundamental value creation effects of learning and responds to basic research issues rather than displaying a potentially complex reality (Burton and Obel, 1995). The model demonstrates a potential to build our understanding of the relationship between market learning, strategic responsiveness, economic performance, and performance risk, as the basic model can be extended in several ways. As such, the simulation model could be modified to explore other aspects of organizational learning. Further studies might examine effects of specific elements of learning, e.g., knowledge creation, unlearning, decay, etc., to develop a more comprehensive understanding of the learning process. Other model extensions might specify how firms can learn through search and experimentation and change market positions through responsive reconfigurations, e.g., product developments, process improvements, service enhancements, etc. Whereas such model refinements can provide a more complete overview of complex strategic adaptation processes, they will not change the fundamental findings reported in this study.

The nature of the study imposes certain limitations on its interpretation. In the simulation model, ex ante market risk is reflected in a stochastic market uncertainty function whereas ex post performance risk is captured by the volatility of the firm's periodic cash flows. This conceptualization of ex ante and ex post risk differs from the risk measures considered in the finance literature where firm specific risk is expressed as the correlation between the market return of a company's stock and the return of a general stock market portfolio (β-coefficient). It is on this basis, the capital asset pricing model stipulates a positive linear relationship between risk (β) and stock market returns (Brealey and Myers, 1994; Sharpe, Alexander and

Bailey, 1999). Whereas other research has disputed the validity of the risk-return relationship implied by the capital assets pricing model (Fama and French, 1992, 1993), the findings reported here do not apply directly to this dispute. However, the study demonstrates that under market uncertainty, learning processes can lead to both higher value creation and lower risk at the same time.

Conclusions

The simulation results indicate that market learning has a positive effect on value creation although optimal learning is achieved well before perfect learning and complete market adaptation. The learning process displays diminishing return characteristics and after the optimal level of learning is reached, higher learning rates reduce value because the incremental revenue gains no longer exceed the required restructuring costs. However, some market learning clearly has a positive effect on value creation, particularly under turbulent market conditions, and simultaneously reduces volatility of cash generation. Hence, market learning leads to an inverse relationship between the net present value and the volatility of the firm's periodic cash flows.

The study introduces a model of market learning that can provide new insights about market conditions and thereby allow the firm to adapt and reconfigure its strategic market position. Simulations on the model demonstrate the basic value creation and risk management effects of learning in environments characterized by different levels of market uncertainty. The simulations demonstrate that market learning can increase the firm's strategic responsiveness and exert a positive influence on the firm's value creation potential while reducing the volatility of periodic cash flows. The model illustrates how market learning and adaptation of the firm's strategic market position can modify potentially disruptive effects of market uncertainty and moderate the firm's ex post performance risk.

References

Alveson, M. (1993). Organizations as Rhetoric: Knowledge-Intensive Firms and the Struggle with Ambiguity. *Journal of Management Studies,* 30, 997-1015.

Argyris, C. and Schön, D. A. (1978). *Organizational Learning: A Theory of Action Perspective.* Addison-Wesley, Reading, MA.

Argyris, C. (1982). *Reasoning, Learning, and Action: Individual and Organizational.* Jossey-Bass, San Francisco.

Barney, J. (1986). Strategic Factor Markets: Expectations, Luck, and Business Strategy. *Management Science,* 32, 1231-1241.

Bateson, G. (1972), *Steps to an Ecology of Mind.* Ballentine Books, New York.

Bettis, R. A. and Hitt, M. A. (1995). The New Competitive Landscape. *Strategic Management Journal,* 16, Special Issue, 7-19.

Bodie, Z., Kane, A. and Marcus, A. J. (1998). *Essentials of Investment,* Third Edition. McGraw-Hill, New York.

Bowman, E. H. (1980). A Risk/Return Paradox for Strategic Management. *Sloan Management Review,* 21, 17-31.

Bowman, E. H. (1982). Risk Seeking by Troubled Firms. *Sloan Management Review,* 23, 33-42.

Bowman, E. H. and Hurry, D. (1993). Strategy Through the Options Lens: An Integrated View of Resource Investments and the Incremental-Choice Process. *Academy of Management Review,* 18, 760-782.

Brealey, R. and Myers, S. (1994). *Principles of Corporate Finance,* Fifth Edition. McGraw-Hill, New York.

Burton, R. M. and Obel, B. (1995). The Validity of Computational Models in Organization Science: From Model Realism to Purpose of the Model. *Computational and Mathematical Organization Theory*, 1, 57-71.

Chatman, J. A. and Barsade, S. G. (1995). Personality, Organizational Culture, and Cooperation: Evidence from a Business Simulation. *Administrative Science Quarterly,* 40, 423-443.

Cyert, R. M. and March, J. G. (1992), *A Behavioral Theory of the Firm*. Second Edition. Blackwell Publishers, Cambridge, MA. (First published in 1963)

D'Aveni R. 1994. *Hypercompetition.* Free Press, New York.

Drucker, P. (1993). *Post-Capitalist Society.* Harper Collins Publishers, New York.

Eisenhardt, K. M. and Martin, J. A. (2000). Dynamic capabilities: What are they? *Strategic Management Journal*, 21, 1105-1121.

Fama, E. F. and French, K. R. (1992). The Cross-Section of Expected Stock Returns. *Journal of Finance,* 47, 427-465.

Fama, E. F. and French, K. R. (1993). Common Risk Factors in Returns on Stocks and Bonds. *Journal of Financial Economics,* 33, 3-56.

Fiol, C. M. and Lyles, M. A. (1985). Organizational Learning. *Academy of Management Journal,* 10, 803-813.

Grant R. M. 1996. Toward a knowledge-based theory of the firm. *Strategic Management Journal*, 17, 109-122.

Hamel, G. and Prahalad, C. K. (1996). Competing in the New Economy: Managing Out of Bounds. *Strategic Management Society,* 16th Annual International Conference.

Huber, G. P. (1991). Organizational Learning: The Contributing Processes and the Literatures. *Organization Science,* 2, 88-115.

Ilinitch, A.Y., D'Avenie, R.A. and Lewin, A.Y. (1996). New Organizational Forms and Strategies for Managing in Hypercompetitive Environments. *Organization Science*, 7, 211-220.

Kiesler, S. and Sproull, L. (1982). Managerial Responses to Changing Environments: Perspectives on Problem Sensing From Social Cognition. *Administrative Science Quarterly,* 27, 548-570.

Klein, J. I. (1989). Parenthetic Learning in Organizations: Toward the Unlearning of the Unlearning Model. *Journal of Management Studies,* 26, 291-308.

Kogut, B. and Zander, U. (1992). Knowledge of the Firm, Combinative Capabilities, and the Replication of Technology. *Organization Science,* 3, 383-397.

Lei, M., Hitt, A. and Bettis, R. A. (1996). Dynamic Core Competences Through Meta-Learning and Strategic Context. *Journal of Management*, 22, 549-569.

Leonard-Barton, D. (1995). *Wellsprings of Knowledge: Building and Sustaining the Sources of Innovation.* Harvard Business School Press, Boston.

Levinthal, D. A. and March, J. G. (1981). A Model of Adaptive Organizational Search. *Journal of Economic Behavior and Organization,* 2, 307-333.

Levinthal, D. A. and March, J. G. (1991). The Myopia of Learning. *Strategic Management Journal,* 14, 95-112.

Lewitt, B. and March, J. G. (1988). Organizational Learning. *Annual Review of Sociology,* 14, 319-340.

Levy, D. (1994). Chaos Theory and Strategy: Theory, Application, and Managerial Implications. *Strategic Management Journal,* Special Issue, 15, 167-178.

Lintner, J. (1965). The Valuation of Risk Assets and the Selection of Risky Investments in Stock Portfolios and Capital Budgets. *Review of Economics and Statistics*, 47, 13-37.

March, J. G. (1991). Exploration and Exploitation in Organizational Learning. *Organization Science,* 2, 71-87.

Nonaka, I. (1994). A Dynamic Theory of Organizational Knowledge Creation. *Organization Science,* 5, 14-37.

Nonaka, I. and Takeuchi, H. (1995). *The Knowledge-Creating Company: How Japanese Companies Create the Dynamics of Innovation.* Oxford University Press, New York.

Nyström, P. C. and Starbuck, W. H. (1984). To Avoid Organizational Crisis, Unlearn. *Organizational Dynamics,* Spring, 53-65.

Prahalad, C. K. and Bettis, R. A. (1986). The Dominant Logic: A New Linkage Between Diversity and Performance. *Strategic Management Journal,* 7, 485-501.

Senge, P. (1990). *The Fifth Discipline: The Art and Practice of the Learning Organization.* Doubleday, New York.

Sharpe, W. F. (1964). Capital Asset Prices: A Theory of Market Equilibrium Under Conditions of Risk. *Journal of Finance,* 19, 425-442.

Sharpe, W. F., Alexander, G. J. and Bailey, J. V. (1999). *Investments.* Sixth Edition. Prentice-Hall, New Jersey.

Sinkula, J. M., Baker, W. E. and Noordewier, T. (1997). A Framework for Market-Based Organizational Learning: Linking Values, Knowledge, and Behavior. *Journal of the Academy of Marketing Science*, 25, 305-318.

Stata, R. (1992). Management Innovation. *Executive Excellence*, 9, 8-9.

Teece, D. J., Pisano, G. and Shuen, A. (1997). Dynamic Capabilities and Strategic Management. *Strategic Management Journal*, 18, 509-534.

CHAPTER 4

Impediments to Effective Risk Management

Peter Winther Schrøder

This paper examines the pattern of risk management practices among Danish companies, identifies the main drivers behind the present practices, and determines critical barriers to adopting a more enterprise-wide risk management approach.

Introduction

The scope of the traditional risk management, which has long been a standard management activity, is limited to risks for which financing is available. These risks are managed disparately in separate units within the company through insurance, financial products (e.g. derivatives), and internal controls aimed to protect the firm against adverse economic effects of risk.

However, corporate misconduct such as witnessed in Enron, Royal Ahold, Parmalat, WorldCom, and Adecco have resulted in growing pressures from corporate governance bodies, including the Danish Nørby Committee; COSO in the US; and legislative initiatives such as the Sarbanes-Oxley Act in the US; for companies to take on greater responsibility in managing (down-side) risk on a more integrated, systematic, and enterprise-wide scale.

On the other hand, several authors emphasize (Liebenberg and Hoyt, 2003; Deloach, 2000; Funston, 2003; Rahardjo and Dowling, 1998; Chapman, 2003; Weber and Liekweg, 2000; COSO, 2003) that risk management is not only to control risks but also to guide growth in the best direction, i.e., consider the opportunistic side of risk. The point is that the companies achieve a better assessment of the magnitude, interaction, and importance of different risks through an Enterprise

Risk Management (ERM) approach[4], which by making risk management a part of the company's business planning process enables them to make better decisions, manage risk in a more active and proactive way and thereby enhance shareholder value. Besides, the required corporate infrastructure enhances flexibility and speed, and increases risk awareness. Consequently, the company is better positioned to move rapidly to exploit risks compared to competitors without the risk management framework.

This article presents both academic and practitioner views on the impediments that exist for implementing effective enterprise risk management programs. This is followed by a description of the methodology used to collect research data. The findings are presented in two main sections respectively addressing present risk management practices and the key barriers to managing risk on a more Enterprise-wide approach. Then the limitations of the study are discussed and the key findings summarized.

Academic and Practitioner Views on Impediments to Effective ERM Programs

The different viewpoints on impediments to implement an effective risk management program are discussed with the aid of McKinseys' 7Ss framework[5]. The framework considers the critical components and the interrelationships between them that a company must take into account when transforming the organization into an enterprise-wide risk management approach.

Several authors (Blacker, 2001; Smiechewicz, 2001; Truslow, 2003; COSO, 2003; Deloach, 2000; Weinstein et al., 2003; Meulbroek, 2002; Barrese, 2003; Dickinson, 2001; Merkeley, 2001; Chapman, 2003; Kayfish, 2001; Kotter, 1995) emphasize that adopting an ERM architecture constitutes a cultural change and the total commitment from the top management including the Board is crucial to a successful ERM programme. The Board must among other things show direction by determining the risk appetite in the entire organization and outlining the risk management policy (Figure 4.1).

---

[4] Enterprise risk management (ERM) can shortly be defined as a holistic, systematic and integrated approach to the management of all key risks and opportunities with the intent of maximizing shareholder value for the enterprise as a whole.

[5] See for instance Sondhi (1999: p. 85).

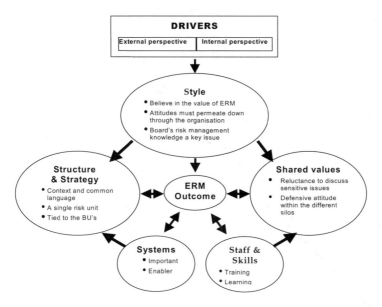

Figure 4.1 Key ERM Issues

However, the lack of risk management knowledge on the Board (Weinstein et al., 2003) and the Board's consensus seeking attitude (Blacker, 2003) may be a key barrier to ERM as it is an impediment to in-depth and open discussions about the company's risks. The executives are ultimately responsible and should assume ownership of the risk-management process in order to ensure buy-in and set the tone for a positive risk culture. Their attitudes must permeate down through the organization aiming at creating a strong and positive risk management culture that ultimately results in the appropriate structure (Chapman, 2001; COSO, 2003).

Yet, a potential barrier to implementing ERM, is according to Merkley (2001), "priority by senior management". Therefore, the success in practice depends on having a visible executive-level champion who really believes in the effort and actively demonstrates support (Chapman 2001; COSO, 2003). However, Kleffner et al.'s (2003) study shows that uncertainty regarding how ERM creates value is one reason why ERM is not more common in practice. Therefore, a strong belief in risk management and clear communication of the value the company seeks from ERM is crucial to establishing a strong risk-robust culture (Schneier and Miccolis, 1998; Barrese and Scordis, 2003; COSO, 2003; Prince, 2000).

Furthermore, reluctance to discuss sensitive issues across the organization caused by a defensive attitude within the different risk silos is a cultural impediment to ERM (Funston, 2003, Blacker, 2003; Kleffner et al., 2003)

A key to successful risk management is a stable and predictable reporting structure that delineates the specific roles and responsibilities to the appropriate personnel in the organization (Weinstein, 2002; Deloach, 2000; Chapman, 2001). However, the more frequent occurrence of looser organizations is a challenge in a risk management context, as the culture in these kinds of organizations is incompatible with the required tight reporting systems (Weinstein, 2002). Nevertheless, the organizational model for ERM is a significant issue as it sets the tone for the culture (Haubenstock, 1999).

The business unit executives must assume primary responsibility for managing risk within their respective areas for ERM to be effective (Truslow, 2003; COSO, 2003; Weber and Liekweg, 2000; Deloach, 2000). However, the complexity of identifying, controlling, and managing risks across a company requires expertise and, therefore, the most effective way to assure continuity and consistency in risk management is with a single organizational unit that bears the responsibility for supervising the full risk management process (Deloach, 2000; Nakada and Tange, 2003; Haubenstock, 1999). This responsibility must go beyond the consultative role in order to ensure real authority. Yet, it may be difficult to implement due to cultural constraints (Deloach, 2000) or the fact that a central role requires knowledge, experience, and a range of skills (Haubenstock, 1999; Sadgrove, 1996).

However, whether it is the Internal Audit or a central Risk Unit that assists in the ERM endeavors, it is essential that they are tied closely to the management team in the various business units in order to be successful as this provides them with a better understanding of the lines of business they support (Truslow, 2003).

Several authors (Froot et al., 1994; Chapman, 2001; Deloach, 2000; COSO, 2003; Smiechewicz, 2001) mention concurrently two critical factors for a successful ERM framework, namely that the risk management strategy is developed coherently with the company's overall strategy and that the risk management activities are integrated in the business processes.

It is hardly surprising that the risk management strategy should be developed coherently with the overall strategy as it ensures alignment between risk strategies, business objectives, and key strategies. If there is no coherence there is a risk, as emphasized by Smiechewicz (2001) that risk management just becomes another form of exercise to complete, or as mentioned by Funston (2003) that risk is interpreted as a negative word that becomes an impediment to progress.

Risks are inherent in all strategic decisions and activities executed by a company. Therefore, the integration of the risk management activities within the business processes is important because risks are best managed and controlled as close as possible to the source of disturbances (Deloach, 2000; COSO, 2003).

Each individual has a different understanding and perspective of the business's risks. Therefore, establishing a common risk universe or language that is customized to the organization's specific needs is vital for an effective risk management across the organization as it ensures a consistent view on risk across the organization. (Deloach, 2000; Chapman, 2001; Smiechewicz, 2001; COSO, 2003).

Difficulties in estimating many of the risks (Kleffner et al., 2003), the scope of the risk analysis (Kleffner et al., 2003), and managers' lack of understanding of simple risk tools (Bologa, 2003; Yu, 2002) are seen by some as barriers to an ERM approach. However, several authors point out that there is too much focus on quantification at the expense of qualitative judgments (Focardi and Jonas, 1998; Martin, 2002), although some form of quantification should support judgments.'

Barrese and Scordis (2003) and Deloach (2000) point out that risk management concepts, applications, and capabilities must be an integral part of the corporate training curriculum. Furthermore, Blacker (2003) emphasizes that training and learning are key factors embedded in the risk management culture. Therefore, organizational and individual learning must support the journey to ERM. In addition, Deloach (2000), Kayfish (2001), and COSO (2003) point out that an effectively functioning ERM environment stimulates the desired behaviors through an appropriate incentive structure.

The lack of quality data, limited access to data due to lack of integration between existing systems, lack of data mapping tools and risk modeling tools are the largest hurdles to an ERM approach (Prince, 2000; Deloach, 2000; Levine, 2004; Chapman, 2003; Liebenberg and Hoyt, 2003). However, Levine (2004) states that many risk management systems still do not present a unified view of the different types of risk, which is hardly surprising as ERM is a very new idea. Prince (2000) emphasizes the importance of systems very clearly: "No matter how good the system is, it still comes down to the people in an organization. The system is an enabler, while people will address the risk."

In light of the above-mentioned key ERM issues this paper's hypothesis is that Danish companies have not embraced enterprise risk management as a modern management discipline due to the lack of commitment from the top management teams including the boards of directors.

Methodology
In order to examine the extent to which ERM is practiced in Denmark and to identify the key ERM issues, a combination of quantitative and qualitative research approaches was pursued.

Questionnaires designed in light of the key issues raised above were chosen as the primary method of collecting information as this approach partly enables to uncover the present risk management behavior in the Danish companies and partly makes it possible to reach a wider audience and thereby collect data from a wide spectrum of industries and company sizes.

A survey was sent to selected organizations among the top 1000 companies plus some smaller companies in Denmark. The profiles of respondents are shown in Appendix one. The total number of surveys sent out was 427. A follow-up letter was sent to non-respondents. Thirty-six valid surveys were returned for a response rate of eight percent.

To gain a deeper understanding of the companies' views on ERM, the author asked the respondents if they would be willing to participate in a telephone interview over about half an hour. Twelve companies were willing to participate in an interview of which 10 were chosen for the exercise. The profiles of the interviewed companies are shown in Appendix one. The interviews addressed specific topics covered through an open-ended discussion although specific questions also were posed in order to fill in important gaps from the respondent's answer to the questionnaire.

In Search for Patterns

Risk Management Practice in Danish Companies
An overall picture of present risk management practices among Danish companies is presented in this section aimed at determining to what extent the Danish companies have embraced enterprise risk management as a modern management discipline. Initially, the key

drivers for the current risk management practices are identified. Afterwards, the extent to which risk management is integrated across the company is mapped. This is followed by a description of the scope of and focus on different types of risk and the approach to manage them. Finally, a conclusion of the present risk management practices is put forward.

Fully 40% of the companies mentioned competitive advantage, cost savings through better management of internal resources, and safeguards against earnings-related surprises as the top three drivers of current risk management practice (Table 4.1).

Nearly one third of the answers can be classified within the category "opportunities" while one half can be classified within the category "protection" and one fifth can be classified within the category "cost-saving". Therefore, the predominant driver behind the present risk management practices is largely protection and cost savings, i.e., defensive in nature.

Category	Motivation	Answer	Answer
Opportunity	Competitive advantage	42%	32%
	Improve business planning	31%	
	Improve capital allocation	14%	
	Improve reputation	11%	
↕	Cost savings through better management of internal resources	44%	19%
	Cost savings through reductions in hedging and insurance costs	11%	
Protection	Safeguard against earnings-related surprises	39%	49%
	Corporate governance guidelines	19%	
	Reduce likelihood of compliance breaches	14%	
	Regulatory pressure	11%	
	Other (protective measures)	21%	

Table 4.1   The Top Three Motivations for Risk Management Practice

It is characteristic of present risk management practices in Denmark that risk management activities are partly integrated across the company (Figure 4.2) as few companies pursue a fully integrated approach. Furthermore, the interviews revealed that the integration takes place within areas such as finance, insurance, IT security, and health & safety, i.e. financial and hazard risks. In continuation of this, approximately half of the companies had built risk management into the planning and decision process. It emerged from the interviews that particularly in matters concerning hazard risks, this practice is predominant. In contrast, strategic risks are incorporated more loosely into the planning and decision process.

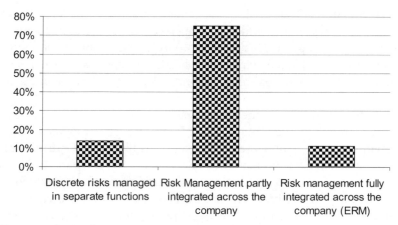

Figure 4.2   Risk Management Integration Across the Company

As a result, there is not a strong coherence between risk management and the overall strategy process in the Danish companies. The observation is hardly surprising due to the fact that the prevalent risk philosophy is protection, i.e., risk management is not seen as an integrated part of creating new business opportunities.

The lack of integration is furthermore reflected in the applied approach to evaluate the risk strategy. Table 4.2 shows that a holistic view leaves much to be desired as only 17% disagree with the statement that risks are evaluated on a stand-alone basis.

Strongly disagree	Disagree	Neither nor	Agree	Strongly agree
3%	14%	33%	44%	3%

Table 4.2   The Extent to Which Risks are Evaluated Individually

The respondents were asked about the range of risks handled in each risk category aimed at determining to what extent the risk management practice was narrowly or broadly focused.

It is evident from Figure 4.3 that financial and hazard risks are investigated and explained to a much larger extent than operational and strategic risks. Thus, all the essential strategic and operational risks are only determined in approximately 15% of the companies. In other words, the risk management practices are rather narrowly focused.

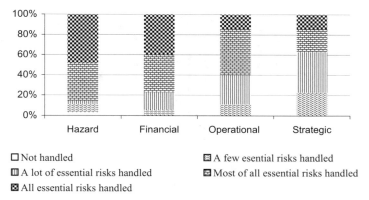

Legend:
☐ Not handled ⊞ A few essential risks handled
Ⅲ A lot of essential risks handled ⊞ Most of all essential risks handled
⊠ All essential risks handled

Figure 4.3   The Range of Risks Handled in Each Risk Category

Furthermore, the survey showed that the companies pursue a much more structured and formal approach when they are dealing with hazard and financial risks compared to operational and especially strategic risks.

In conclusion, the Danish companies have not embraced ERM as a modern management discipline. The present risk management practices are rather narrowly focused as priority is given to the management of financial and hazard risks, which may be attributed to the fact that the predominant motivation for risk management is largely protection and cost-savings, i.e., rather defensive by nature. Hence, these risks are scrutinized in a much more structured and formal manner and explained to a much lager extent than operational and strategic risks. Therefore, there is still a long journey to go as only few companies try to pursue a fully integrated approach. As a result, risks and risk strategies are to a large extent evaluated on a stand-alone basis. Consequently, a holistic view on risk management among the Danish companies still leaves much to be desired.

Key barriers to Managing Risk on a More Enterprise-Wide Approach

Overview
The two most important barriers to more enterprise-wide risk management practices are the lack of a common language and low recognition of potential benefits (Figure 4.4).

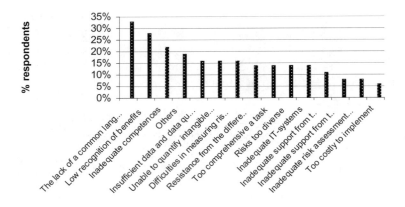

Figure 4.4   Main Barriers to Manage Risk on an Enterprise-Wide Scale

It appears from the figure that factors related to the risk management process, e.g. a common language, competences, data quality, and measuring & quantification systems, are more frequently mentioned as a barrier compared to the cultural aspects, such as, resistance within the organization and inadequate support from top-management and the board of directors.

Low Recognition of the Benefits

"Low benefits" is the most important barrier. As a matter of fact 40%[6] of the companies in the survey state that a low recognition of the benefits is the major barrier to assuming a more enterprise-wide risk management approach, indicating that present practices of managing risks are sufficient. However, it appears from Figure 4.5 that the strategic risks are considered nearly twice as important as financial and hazard risks. Therefore, it is surprising that the management of strategic risks has received less attention and is managed more informally. Although it is possible to manage risks properly even with an ad-hoc approach, analyses performed in the United States by MMC Research[7] show that more than 90% of the 100 largest one-month drops in shareholder value could be attributed to a strategic or an

---

[6] Nearly nine percent of all respondents mentioned under the category "others" that "unfavorable cost/reward from ERM", "cost-benefit considerations" and "prioritization of resources" as a cause. These motives are closely linked to a low recognition of the benefits.

[7] See http://www.casact.org/coneduc/rcm/2002/handouts/wolf2.ppt

operational event[8]. Furthermore, their findings show that two thirds of these risks could be anticipated and mitigated through the use of known tools and techniques. In other words, they indicate that a proactive management of strategic and operational risks can add value and therefore should get more attention.

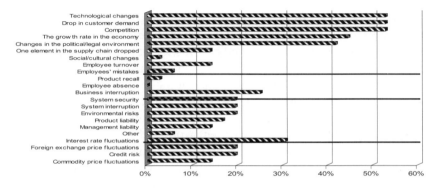

Figure 4.5   The Importance of Different Risks

Strategy

The lack of a common risk management language is stated as the second most important barrier to a more enterprise-wide risk management supporting the argument put forward in the literature that a common language is vital for an effective risk management across the organization. However, a common language is to a large extent a question about defining and describing the relevant risks. So, why should language become an important barrier? It may be caused by the present rather narrow-minded risk awareness orientation focused mainly on financial and hazard risks and, therefore, it appears overwhelming to start looking at all risks, cf. the scope barrier argument presented by Kleffner et al. (2003).

The accessibility of practical tools and understanding simple risk techniques is in contrast to the theoretical arguments not seen as critical barriers to ERM. As a matter of fact, risk tools are widely distributed and applied in the companies' risk assessment activities. Thus, nearly half the companies use assessment interviews and/or workshops to identify the risks and use risk mapping to graduate the different risks. Similarly, difficulties in quantifying and measuring risks across the organization are not seen as a major barrier to ERM in

---

[8] A similar study does not exist on Danish companies.

the Danish companies. This is hardly surprising due to the companies' widespread use of risk mapping simultaneously with their focus on qualitative aspects, which is in keeping with the recommendations in the literature.

Style and Shared Values

Inadequate support from the board of directors is not seen as an important barrier to managing risks on a more enterprise-wide basis. At first, this seems to be supported by the fact that the board approves and reviews the company's risk policies and procedures in nearly 80% of the companies. However, the interviews revealed that the risk policies and procedures cover insurance, financial, and IT-security risks in 7 cases out of 10. Only one company mentioned that they have clear policies for all risks. In other words, the risk policies and procedures are primarily limited to financial and hazard risks.

The board of directors sets the company's risk appetite for the different risks to a varying degree. Furthermore, the board looks at the different risks separately in the majority of the companies, an observation in line with the observed partly integrated risk management practice (Figure 4.2). Similarly, the board only details the risk appetite in the entire organization to a limited extent.

All in all, the board of directors supports the risk management activities as all types of risks are treated in the boardroom although to varying degrees, but no holistic view on risks is taken. Therefore, although the board supports risk management, it does not show a commitment to an enterprise-wide approach.

The evolution of risk management practices among Danish companies is so closely linked to historical events[9] that the author doubts that the boards' lack of commitment to ERM is a conscious evaluation of the pros and cons. On the contrary, the lack of knowledge as emphasized by Higgs in Weinstein et al. (2003) is probably the explanation. This hypothesis is supported by the interviews, which showed that the boards' examination of risks was ad hoc or performed once a year, indicating a compliance/check-list approach to risk management. In other words, the boards of directors must become more knowledgeable about ERM.

---

[9] Focus on hazard due to a demand from the insurance companies; emergence of virus etc has raised the attention to IT-security; EMS breakdown in 1992 resulted in enhanced awareness about financial risks.

According to the survey, the top executives believe in the risk management efforts across the organization in nearly 60% of the companies (Table 4.3).

		The top-executives really believe in the risk management efforts across the organization and actively demonstrate their support				
		Strongly disagree	Disagree	Neither nor	Agree	Strongly agree
	All	6%	20%	17%	43%	14%
Decisions to transfer or accept risks are mainly evaluated on a stand alone basis	Strongly disagree	50%	0%	0%	0%	0%
	Disagree	0%	0%	0%	27%	20%
	Neither nor	50%	29%	33%	40%	20%
	Agree	0%	57%	67%	33%	60%
	Strongly agree	0%	14%	0%	0%	0%
	Total	2	7	6	15	5

Table 4.3   The Top-Executives' Support

However, there is little coherence between the top-executives' support of risk management across the organization and the way the companies approach their risk strategies. If the commitment implies a holistic view on risk management, it would be expected that a majority of the answers were distributed around the 'boxed' diagonal in Table 4.3. In fact, there is a clear indication that low commitment implies risk evaluations on a stand-alone basis. Conversely, only one company out of four[10] that believes in risk management across the organization demonstrates this by adopting a more holistic approach to their risk strategies. In other words, while there is a focus on risks and they are discussed, it does not take place from a holistic point of view.

In addition, there is a distinct tendency to be frank about risk in the companies as learning from past mistakes, knowledge sharing, and open communication is prevalent in eight companies out of ten. Nevertheless, the survey indicates that risk awareness has a low priority in the companies as training in the organization's attitude toward risk is important in only a third of the companies. However, this is not a surprise in light of the low commitment mentioned above since change must be driven from the top.

All in all, although the majority of the top executives support the risk management efforts across the organization only a few demonstrate this by incorporating a more holistic approach in their risk strategies and using training to support the organization's risk attitude.

---

[10] Derived as follows: $(27*43 + 20*14)/57 = 25.28$ ($\cong 25\%$).

It is an obvious conclusion that the executives' lack of support to ERM is caused by uncertainty about how ERM creates value, as mentioned by Kleffner et al. (2003) and, therefore, ERM has low priority (Merkley, 2001). On the other hand, companies that practice ERM successfully, as exemplified by two of the interviewed companies, have their top management teams and boards of directors focusing on risks continuously, assuming direct ownership of the risk management process, and believing in risk awareness and learning as important parts of the training curriculum, all in keeping with the stated elements for success (Chapman, 2001; COSO, 2003).

All in all, the general lack of top management and board commitment among the Danish companies to an ERM approach can be attributed to the barriers mentioned in the literature. On the other hand, companies practicing ERM successfully are pursuing the recommendations as developed in the theory.

Structure

The Finance Departments are responsible for risk management in the majority of the companies as they are directly or indirectly in charge of risk assessments in 70% of the companies (Figure 4.6). Consequently, the Danish companies organize their risk management predominantly through stable reporting structures with reporting to the CEO or another senior officer, in line with the recommendations established by different authors.

However, the structure is limited to areas where the risk management process has a focus mainly in the areas of financial and hazard risks. The interviews showed that the organization of strategic and operational risks is much more loosely structured, which is consistent with the fact that these risks receive less attention.

Figure 4.6   Risk Management in the Organizational Structure

The survey shows that the management of business risks is left in the hands of the business units (Table 4.4), a practice in keeping with the recommendations from the literature. However, the responsibility for the measurement, controlling, and reporting of these risks differs according to the types of structure. It is a fact that delegation is more pronounced in informal structures than formal ones supporting Weinstein's (2002) argument that looser organizations are incompatible with the requirement for tightly reporting systems.

	Intrapreneurial	Entrepreneurial	Delegative	Regimented	All
The risk measurement	57%	71%	25%	23%	40%
The risk control	57%	57%	25%	31%	40%
The risk reporting	57%	71%	38%	38%	49%
Managing risks	86%	71%	88%	77%	80%
Number of firms	7	7	8	13	35
NB: Definitions are described in appendix 2					

Table 4.4   The Decentralized Handling of Business Risks

The viewpoint advanced by Deloach (2000), Nakada and Tange (2003) and Haubenstock (1999) that a single organizational unit must bear the responsibility for supervising the entire risk management process in order to ensure continuity and consistency effectively is fully supported and practiced by two interviewed ERM-companies. However, other companies put forward enhanced bureaucracy and the elimination of business units' independence as arguments against centralization.

All the interviewed companies' risk management units play a consultative role in line with a lot of authors' viewpoints but contrary to Haubenstock's (1999) emphasis on the risk manager having a managerial role. A risk manager in an ERM-company may reflect the motive captured by the comment: "We are good at ensuring alignment, counseling, elaborating guidelines, and reviewing the framework. The risk ownership is carried out by those people in the company with an in-depth knowledge about the specific risks." This remark is to some extent in line with Haubenstock's (1999) and Sadgrove's (1996) reservations about a single point of responsibility, namely that it requires knowledge, experience, and skills. Hence, COSO's (2003) and Deloach's (2000) viewpoint that the risk management function will be most successful when it is set up as a staff function to provide support, facilitation, and co-ordination to line management, is seemingly supported by the practice in the Danish companies.

Furthermore, the risk management function is not closely tied to the business no matter what risk management practice is pursued, a condition that according to Truslow (2003) is crucial for success. However, the survey may in this specific case reflect emotional attitudes. Staff functions operate as advisors and, therefore, it is a challenge to be considered as an integrated member of the management team in the different businesses. Conversely, the advisor may still have in-depth understanding of the business and contribute successfully to a company's ERM efforts. Hence, the decisive factor for success is knowledge rather than an integrated membership of the management team.

Staff, Skills and Systems

Training in attitudes to risk is, contrast to theoretical arguments, not an important element in the companies' training and learning cycles, which may be due to the fact that risk awareness has a low priority among the Danish companies.

The use of learning and knowledge sharing has gained ground in the Danish companies, elements that some authors find vital for effective risk management. However, the author doubts that the proliferation is specifically related to risk management as risk awareness is low on the list of priorities. If anything, it is a general trend in the application of learning and knowledge sharing in the Danish companies.

In contrast to the recommendations extracted from the literature, few Danish companies have incentive systems that are aligned with risk objectives. This finding is hardly surprising as risk awareness is low on the list of priorities and accordingly the importance of proper risk behavior has less emphasis.

Lack of data, system integration, and technological tools are frequently mentioned in the literature as barriers to the proliferation of ERM. However, the analysis of the Danish companies shows that systems are only a minor barrier. This may be explained by the fact that the Danish risk management practices are only partly integrated and mainly focused on traditional risks where systems are available.

Limitations of the Research

The fact that only 36 companies answered the survey, corresponding to a response rate of eight percent, means that the statistical uncertainty, all other things being equal, remains large. On the other hand, the tendencies are quite consistent across the respondents, which reduce possible biases in the conclusions.

Furthermore, the sample is not sufficiently representative of different types of companies operating in the Danish economy. There are too few respondents among companies with less than 200 employees, cf. Appendix one. In contrast, companies with more than 200 employees are plentifully represented. A cross section of different industries are to a large extent represented satisfactorily in the sample, although no conclusions can be drawn regarding the energy and construction industry since they are not included in the sample.

A major challenge with surveys is that they may actually count attitudes and not deeds. However, the interviews to a great extent supported the findings from the survey indicating that the answers give a fair picture of the companies' present practice. Nonetheless, it appeared from the interviews that the respondents interpreted the questions differently from the author's intentions in some instances. Finally, the fact that nearly one third of the respondents have no direct relation to risk management may have affected the answers in a one-sided direction due to lack of deep insights. Hence, the tendencies reflected in the findings, although quite consistent, may need some moderation.

On the whole, the study provides a basis for drawing some conclusions with regards to Danish companies with more than 200 employees excluding companies in the energy and construction industries. The fit between the answers in the survey and the adjacent interviews validates the findings although some biases without a doubt remain. However, the author is confident that the reported tendencies provide a good reflection of current practices.

Summary

The collected data support the hypothesis that Danish companies have not embraced enterprise risk management as a modern management discipline due to the lack of commitment from the top management team including the boards of directors.

The risk management process is not fully integrated across the organization but varies across the types of risk. The management of financial and hazard risks is integrated across the companies in a structured, in-depth, and formal way in the majority of the companies, while strategic risks are treated rather loosely. Indeed, only a few companies pursue a fully integrated approach.

The boards of directors as well as the CEOs support the risk management activities in the companies. However, their focus and attention varies across the different types of risks and each risk type is predominantly treated separately. As a result, although the board and top management support risk management activities across the organization, they do not show a commitment to engage in an enterprise-wide approach. Whether the low commitment is the result of a deliberate choice cannot be determined but it is a fact that the most frequently mentioned barrier to a more enterprise-wide risk management approach is low recognition of the benefits.

Other research shows that managing strategic and operational risks within an ERM framework could create further value indicating that the lack of commitment to enterprise-wide risk management can be attributed to a lack of knowledge as mentioned in the literature rather than a conscious evaluation of the pros and cons of ERM. Likewise, the executives' lack of support for ERM is rooted in uncertainty about how ERM creates value, low priority, and barriers frequently mentioned in the literature. On the other hand, companies practicing ERM successfully are pursuing the recommendations prescribed in the literature. They have visible top management teams and boards of directors focused on the risk management process in words and in deeds. Cultural barriers such as specialized silos are eliminated by in-depth knowledge of the business, involving the business units in the elaboration of the framework, and not least in convincing them how the change can add value.

There is hardly any coherence between risk management and the overall business strategy among the Danish companies, which may be attributed to the fact that the prevalent risk philosophy is protection. On the other hand, Danish ERM-practitioners align risk management with strategic objectives fully in keeping with the recommendations in the literature.

The risk culture environment is overall positive and proactive with a considerable frankness about risks, learning from mistakes and a low presence of silo mentality. However, although the use of learning and knowledge sharing has gained ground in the Danish companies, it is probably a general trend in the application and not a practice specifically related to risk management. In fact, risk awareness generally has a low priority in the companies.

The Danish companies to a large extent organize risk management as prescribed in the literature. In accordance with theory, the findings show that the responsibility for the handling of different aspects of business risks varies according to the type of organizational structure. However, the practices in some Danish ERM-companies show that delegation of responsibility is possible and compatible with the recommendations by different authors that a single organizational unit must bear the responsibility for supervising the entire risk management process.

Theory and the empirical findings underscore that an unambiguous definition and description of the different risks across the organization, i.e., assuming a common language, is vital for the implementation of ERM. However, the fact that the lack of a common language is seen as the second most important barrier to ERM in the Danish companies is surprising as it is a matter of definitions and accordingly can be implemented by starting up on a small scale in cooperation with key risk holders.

The barriers to ERM frequently mentioned in the literature such as the accessibility of practical tools, understanding of simple techniques, and difficulties in quantifying risks across the organization, are not considered a problem in the Danish companies as they are familiar with the use of different tools and techniques.

Peter Winther Schrøder

	Population*)	Respondents	Interviews
Industries			
Manufacturing	13%	28%	30%
Electricity, gas and water supply	0.4%	0%	0%
Construction	8%	0%	0%
Wholesale and retail trade, hotels, restaurants	26%	14%	20%
Transport, post and telecommunication	6%	25%	30%
Financial intermediation/services	3%	11%	10%
Other Business service	10%	22%	10%
Public and personal services	35%	0%	0%
Other	0%	0%	0%
Number of employees			
10-19	52%	3%	0%
20-49	31%	3%	10%
50-99	10%	6%	0%
100-199	4%	3%	0%
200-499	2%	22%	10%
500+	1%	64%	80%
Position in the organisation			
CFO		22%	20%
CRO		0%	0%
CAO		0%	0%
Financial Manager		22%	20%
Risk Manager		14%	40%
Audit Manager		0%	0%
CEO/MD		11%	10%
Other		31%	10%

*) Source: Statistics Denmark, Statistiske efterretninger: Generel Erhvervsstatistik, 2004:13 27 July 2004.

Appendix 1   The Profiles of Respondents and Interviewees

Processes / Decision making	Formal	Informal
Centralised	**Regimented**	**Entrepreneurial**
Decentralised	**Delegative**	**Intrapreneurial**

Appendix 2   The Definition of Structure Types

References

Barrese, J. and Scordis, N. (2003). Corporate Risk Management. *Review of Business*, 24 (3), 26-29.

Blacker, K. (2001). The difficulty and importance of managing risk. Henley Management College.

Blacker, K. (2003). People risk and organisational culture: a case study. Henley Management College.

Bologa, J. (2003). Focus on Risk Management. *Internal Auditor*, 60 (4), 9.
Chapman, C. (2001). The Big Picture. *Internal Auditor*, 58 (3), 30-37.

Chapman, C. (2003). Bringing ERM Into Focus. *Internal Auditor*, 60 (3), 30-35.

COSO (2003). Committee of Sponsoring Organizations of Tradeway Commission. Enterprise Risk management Framework. *Available at http://www.erm.coso.org*

Deloach, J. W. (2000). *Enterprise-Wide Risk Management: Strategies for Linking Risk and Opportunity*. Financial Times Prentice Hall, London.

Dickinson, G. (2001). Enterprise Risk Management: Its Origins and Conceptual Foundation. *Geneva Papers on Risk & Insurance*, 26 (3), 360-366.

Focardi, S. and Jonas, C. (1998). *Risk management: Framework, methods, and practice*. Frank J. Fabozzi Associates, Pennsylvania, US.

Froot, K. A., Scharfstein, D. S., Stein, J. C. (1994). A Framework for Risk Management. *Harvard Business Review*, 72 (6), 91-102.

Funston, R. (2003). Creating a Risk-intelligent Organization. *Internal Auditor*, 60 (2), 59-63.

Haubenstock, M. (1999). Organizing a financial institution to deliver enterprise-wide risk management. The Journal of Lending & Credit *Risk Management*, 81 (6), 46-52.

Kayfish, L. (2001). ERM Advice from the Pioneers. *Risk Management*, 48 (10), 64.

Kleffner, A. E., Lee, R. B. and McGannon, B. (2003). The Effect of Corporate Governance on the Use of Enterprise Risk Management: Evidence From Canada. *Risk Management & Insurance Review*, 6 (1), 53-73.

Kotter, J. P. (1995). Leading change: why transformation efforts fail. *Harvard Business Review*, 73 (2), 59-67.

Levine, R. (2004). Risk Management Systems: Understanding the need. *Information Systems Management*, 21 (2), 31- 37.

Liebenberg, A. P., Hoyt, R. E. (2003). The Determinants of Enterprise Risk Management: Evidence From the Appointment of Chief Risk Officers. *Risk Management & Insurance Review*, 6 (1), 37-52.

Martin, P. (2002). Taming Uncertainty. *The RMA Journal*, 85 (1), 58-59.

Merkley, B. W. (2001). Does Enterprise Risk Management Count? *Risk Management*, 48 (4), 25-27.

Meulbroek, L. K. (2002). Integrated Risk Management for the Firm: A Senior Manager's Guide. *Available at http://www.hbs.edu/research/ facpubs/ workingpapers/papers2/0102/02-046.pdf*

Nakada, P. and Tange, C. (2003). The Risk Management of War versus Decentralized Control. *The RMA Journal*, 85 (6), 30-31

Prince, M. (2000). Enterprise risk management; RMIS requires corporate cultural transformation. *Business Insurance*, 34 (49), 21-23

Rahardjo, K. and Dowling, M. A. (1998). A Broader Vision: Strategic risk management. *Risk Management*, 45 (9), 44-49

Sadgrove, K. (1996). *The Complete Guide to Business Risk Management*. Grower, London

Schneier, R. and Miccolis, J. (1998). Enterprise risk management. *Strategy & Leadership*, 26 (2), 10-14

Smiechewicz, W. (2001). Case Study: Implementing Enterprise Risk Management. *Bank Accounting & Finance*, 14 (4), 21-27

Sondhi, R. K. (1999). *Total Strategy*. Airworthy Publications International Limited, Great Britain.

Truslow, D. K. (2003). Operational Risk Management: It's Everyone's Job. *The RMA Journal*, 85 (5), 34-37

Weber, J. and Liekweg, A. (2000). Statutory Regulation of the Risk-Management Function In Germany: Implementation Issues for the Non-Financial Sector, in Frenkel, M., Hommel, U. and Rudolf, M. *Risk Management: Challenge and Opportunity*. Springer, Berlin, 277-294.

Weinstein, B. (2002). Risk Management versus The Loose Organisation. Working Paper, Henley Management College. *Available at http://www.henleymc.ac.uk/henleyres03.nsf/pages/hcvi*

Weinstein, B., Blacker, K. and Mills, R. (2003). Risk management for non-executive directors: creating a culture of cautious innovation. Henley Discussion Paper no. 2. *Available at http://www.henleymc.ac.uk/henleyres03.nsf/pages/hcvi*

Yu, L. (2002). Risk Management in Practice. *MIT Sloan Management Review*, 44 (1), 9.

CHAPTER 5

Risk and Complexity in Social Systems: The Case of the "Business Risk Audit"

Kim Klarskov Jeppesen

When the greatest risk to value is not what has gone wrong, but what could go wrong, you need a forward looking, risk-based approach to provide reliable assurance.

Arthur Andersen, 2001

Quote from Arthur Andersen's home page, 5th December 2001. On June 15th 2002 the firm was convicted for obstruction of justice following the massive shredding of documentation related to Enron. By then it had literally disintegrated.

Introduction

The last five years have been rather turbulent times for the audit industry. Following the Enron debacle, audit firm Arthur Andersen[11] collapsed within months as well. Enron was not a single mishap but followed a number of major fraud cases among Arthur Andersen clients in the late 1990's. The Waste Management-case, which followed the Sunbeam and Baptist Foundation of Arizona fraud cases, led the Securities and Exchange Commission (SEC) to fine Arthur Andersen $7 million and deny four Andersen partners the right to audit SEC-registered clients. At the same time Arthur Andersen was warned that if they were again found guilty of improper professional conduct, the SEC would deny the firm the right to audit SEC-registered companies. Then came Enron, WorldCom, Global Crossing and a

---

[11] By the beginning of 2001 Arthur Andersen (or simply Andersen as it had renamed itself by that time) was the worlds fifth largest audit firm with an annual revenue in 2000 of $8,400 million (see International Accounting Bulletin, Issue 280, December 2000).

number of minor cases, which left an impression of systematic negligence that sealed Andersen's fate. However, the problem of audit firm negligence is not restricted to the USA or to Arthur Andersen. Shortly after Enron a number of similar high profile cases appeared in Europe involving other audit firms. Royal Ahold in the Netherlands involving KPMG, Parmalat in Italy involving Grant Thornton and Deloitte & Touche, and Equitable Life in the UK involving Ernst & Young all point to the universality of the problem, albeit the involved audit firms seem to survive these cases.

These audit failures have all occurred shortly after the audit firms completed a re-engineering of their audit approaches into what has later become known as "business risk audits" [12]. A number of writers such as Bell et al. (1997), Bell and Solomon (2002), Lemon et al. (2000), and Eilifsen et al. (2001) have all described the business risk audit (BRA) approach in details. Generally these approaches consist of three steps. First a strategic analysis is conducted in which the auditor gains an understanding of the entity's business, the strategic business risks facing the entity, and the strategic controls management has put in place to respond to these risks. Second, the key business processes are identified along with the risks threatening the processes and the operational controls management has put in place to ensure that the entity responds to emerging risks. Third, additional audit evidence is collected, mainly by various analytical procedures such as financial and operational benchmarking.

Using the business risk audit concept as its case, the purpose of this paper is to analyze how the perception of business risk is affected by the degree of complexity in the social system that the business is part of. To do so, the next section starts by showing how business risk audits are conceptually founded in systems theory and go on to outline the practice of auditing. In the subsequent section Charles Perrow's theory of risk in systems is introduced. Based on this theoretical approach the following section analyzes how the transition into business risk audits affects the business risk of the audit firms. The final section discusses the perspectives for risk analysis in general.

---

[12] Apparently Arthur Andersen led the way with their approach, ambiguously called "The Business Audit", which was developed from around 1991 and implemented in 1997 (Toffler, 2003: 132). Ernst & Young started their "Audit Innovation" project around 1994 and KPMG followed with their "Business Measurement Process" from around 1996. Later PricewaterhouseCoopers appears to have adopted the BRA approach as well (Winograd et al., 2000). Andersen's "Business Audit" was widely seen as the most radical of these concepts.

The System of Auditing

Viewing the client through a 'strategic-systems lens' the business risk audit concept is explicitly based on systems theory (Bell et al., 1997: 14-24) where a system is defined as a collection of parts that interact to function as a whole. In such a system, business risk deals with the strength of the connections between the organization and its environment. Since the product or service sold by the firm inevitably constitutes one of the main connections, any change of a product directly affects the business risk. When auditing is re-engineered a change in risk exposure should therefore be expected.

To analyze such changes in risk exposure the first step is to outline the system of auditing. Michael Power (1997: 36-39) analyses the system of financial auditing knowledge and presents a meta-system consisting of four elements or subsystems as shown in Figure 5.1.

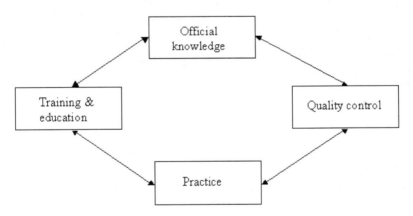

Source: Power (1997: 36).
Figure 5.1   The audit system

The first element is the official knowledge of what constitutes generally accepted practice as described by, for instance auditing standards. In the second element official knowledge is disseminated to practice by the educational system and by the socialization that takes place in the audit firms. The third element is the quality control system, which ensures that the official knowledge is actually followed by the audit firms, making auditing practice, the fourth element, in accordance with the official knowledge. Together the four elements form a system, which is easily controllable by the profession and in which system failures can be explained as individual failures requiring more and better auditing.

Each of the four elements or subsystems is made up of a number of fairly complex parts. The audit practice subsystem of an audit firm, which is the focus of this paper, consists of a number of audit engagements with particular clients. Since the business risk audit concept views the client as a complex web of interrelationships (see Figure 5.2) each engagement, therefore, has an individual and fairly complex risk profile.

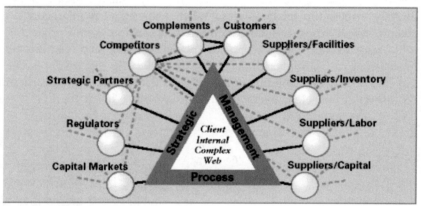

Source: Bell et al. (1997: p. 19).
Figure 5.2   The client as a complex web of interrelationships

Although not indicated in the figure, the audit firm itself is obviously also part of this subsystem because unqualified audit reports are needed when the clients acquire capital and facilitate cooperation with suppliers. Beyond the system is the environment that constitutes everything that is not part of the system. In the audit case this may for instance be the public opinion often represented or given voice by journalists. Since the environment has a more or less legitimate interest in the system, and often tries to become part of it, it makes the boundary between the system and the environment somewhat vague. This is what distinguishes technological systems from social systems and makes analysis of risk in the latter particularly difficult.

Perrow's Theory of Risk in Systems

According to the theory of risk in systems presented by Perrow (1984/1999) under the heading *Normal Accident Theory,* a system is made up of three underlying levels: subsystems, units, and parts. In the theory, an accident is the failure of a subsystem, or the system as a whole, that disrupts the output of the system. Perrow's great contribution to risk analysis is the discovery that the risk of such failures happening is directly affected by the coupling between the parts in the system and the way they interact with each other.

To start with the latter, the parts in the system may interact in a linear or complex way. Linear interaction is sequential or serial step-by-step interaction, where one part or unit of the system interacts with another that follows it immediately in a planned production sequence. If failures occur in the line of interaction these are easily located and parts or people are easily substituted. Furthermore, the processes are well understood making the location and consequences of potential failures highly predictable. Linear interaction is therefore easily controlled centrally.

Complex interaction, on the other hand, is found where the parts of the system interact with components outside the normal production sequence in unintended ways. This may for instance be the result of common mode connections, where parts have multiple functions in different subsystems thereby connecting them. It may also be the result of unintended feedback loops, where errors and failures are not reported to the right place. It may be the result of operators misinterpreting the failure information they get as being within the routine fluctuations, or operators failing to understand the complexity of the control system that is needed in complex systems. Finally, it may simply be the result of proximity, either proximity of subsystems causing them to interact, or proximity between subsystems and the environment. Since complex interaction is by nature unpredictable, it cannot easily be controlled centrally but requires a decentralized control system.

The last dimension in Perrow's approach to systems risk analysis is the coupling between the elements in the system, which may be loose or tight. In loosely coupled systems changes in subsystems or in the environment affect the system indirectly and slowly, thereby leaving plenty of time to react to the change, for instance by replacing equipment, changing the order of sequences, or finding alternative methods. Loosely coupled systems are consequently able to withstand shocks and failures without immediate destabilization but this flexibility is bought at the price of relative inefficiency. Because of the built in slack, loosely coupled systems are manageable by centralized as well as decentralized control approaches.

In tightly coupled systems, on the other hand, there is no such slack built into the system. Tightly coupled systems are lean production systems, highly efficient and time-dependent in their invariant processes. Changes in one subsystem or in the environment will immediately affect the entire system. Buffers, redundancies, and substitutions are only possible to the extent they are designed into the process. Since there is very little time to react to failures a centrally planned control approach is needed. To sum up, what Perrow suggests is, therefore, to categorize systems according to the 2x2 matrix shown in Figure 5.3.

	Interaction	
	Linear	Complex
Tight	Possible failures are predictable, and directly affect the system. Although consequences of failure may be grave, linear interaction makes risk easily controllable by centrally planned controls. Risk is therefore medium in these systems.	Possible failures are unpredictable and directly affect the system. Inherent risk in the system is high and not easily controllable, since the tight coupling requires a centralised control approach whereas the complexity requires decentralised control approach.
Loose	Possible failures re predictable and does not directly affect the system. These systems may easily be controlled centrally as well as decentrally and is therefore low on risk.	Possible failures are unpredictable but does not directly affect the system. Inherent risk in these systems are therefore medium and is best controlled by decentralised strategies.

(Coupling)

Source: Based on Perrow (1984/1999: figure 3.1 & 9.2).
Figure 5.3 Perrow's classification of risk in systems

The Business Risk of Audits

To analyze the business risk of audits according to Perrow's systems approach, a distinction between the old audit risk model[13] and business risk audit must be made. Traditional audits following the audit risk model are usually highly structured. The audit risk model was a product of the late 1980's where a highly structured audit process was generally seen as necessary to reduce costs, reduce uncertainty and ambiguity in the audit process, keep the growing audit firms under centralized control, and protect it against litigation (Knechel, 2005;

---

[13] Audit risk is the risk that auditors give an inappropriate audit opinion when the financial statements are materially misstated. Audit risk consists of three components: inherent risk (the risk that material misstatements occur), control risk (that the internal control system does not detect material misstatements), and detection risk (that audit procedures do not detect material misstatements).

Power, 2003). Structure was initially defined by Cushing and Loebbecke (1986) as: "a systematic approach to auditing characterized by a prescribed, logical sequence of procedures, decisions, and documentation steps, and by a comprehensive and integrated set of audit policies and tools designed to assist the auditor in conducting the audit". In other words, the structured audit process was an attempt to reduce the professional judgments that made the audit process heterogeneous within the big audit firms, thereby reducing the perceived business risk that followed this. As the definition of structure clearly shows, the way to reduce this risk was to impose a centrally controlled, sequential or linear audit process.

In the same way the ideal client is seen as a linear interacting "mechanistic" system of business procedures and internal controls, although it has been argued that there are many advantages for auditors in applying a more complex "organic" view of the client (Dirsmith and McAllister, 1982). Nevertheless, the audit strategy has alternatives built in. If for instance systems auditing is not possible, the auditor will fall back on substantive testing. In addition, the chosen audit procedures/tests may easily be replaced by alternative tests if for some reason they cannot be carried out. Furthermore, a good deal of the audit work is done before year-end making processing delays possible and allowing a certain slack in the required resources. In other words, the coupling between the elements in the traditional audit is highly substitutable and fairly loose.

The highly structured audit risk model is therefore characterized by loose coupling and linear interaction, which makes it a fairly low risk system according to Perrow's classification. Furthermore, the involved risk is easy to control. Linear interaction is usually controlled well by centralized procedures and loose coupling is manageable by centralization as well as decentralization. The centralized control within the traditional audit process in the form of structured processes, audit manuals, auditing standards, and peer review, therefore, worked reasonably well in terms of controlling the audit firm. In addition to being an audit-planning model, the structured audit risk model is, therefore, also a management control system (Power, 2003: 381).

Being a management control system dressed up as an audit planning approach, the audit risk model has been relatively successful. Being focused on internal use, the model nevertheless has inherent problems when used externally, which soon after the models introduction was revealed by expectation gap studies (see for instance Humphrey, 1997). The audit risk model tends to ostracize certain user groups from the system to the environments and the expectation gap studies revealed a high degree of dissatisfaction among these constituents (see for instance Humphrey, 1997), in particular with the way auditors renounced responsibility for detecting fraud and going concern[14] problems. The auditors' strategy to deal with this dissatisfaction was to inform and educate the public about the limitations of auditing. However, as it became clear that this strategy was not going to work pressure was on the profession to expand the audit system to include responsibility for finding material (management) fraud and for detecting going concern problems at an early stage. To do so the auditor needed a thorough understanding of the clients business rather than just the financial statements. Evaluation of management's competencies and integrity as well as a general understanding of the business risks facing the client, therefore, became the foundation of business risk audits.

However, this expansion in the scope of auditing also changes the audit system and the inherent business risk of auditing. In Figure 5.4 an overview of KPMG's business risk audit approach is presented. The model is circular with no clear beginning or end and each unit directly affects the others. The business model also gives input to other audit subsystems, such as the yearly client retention decision. Parts of the model thereby have "common-mode" functions, i.e., they give input to multiple other parts or subsystems. Common-mode functions are according to Perrow a typical source of system complexity since it makes failures in one part of the system spread throughout it often in unpredictable ways. Furthermore, in business risk audits planning is no longer just about finding a cost-effective way to do the audit but also about finding ways to expand revenue by selling more consulting services (Jeppesen, 1998). The tools to expand consulting are an audit of the business strategy and related controls and of the performance of key business processes and process controls with the possibility of giving business advice on perceived performance gaps.

---

[14] Under the going concern assumption, the entity is seen as continuing its business in the foreseeable future, and assets and liabilities are recorded on the basis that this is the case. The time horizon for which auditors are now required to assess going concern for an entity is 12 months.

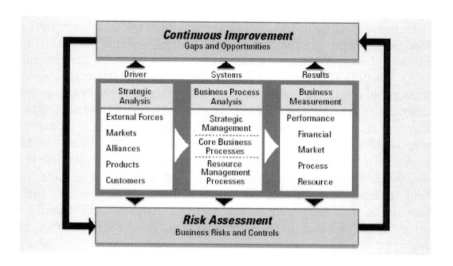

Source: Bell et al. (1997: p. 34).

Figure 5.4   The KPMG Business Measurement Process

Auditing thereby becomes part of good management practice in general and corporate risk management in particular. This broadening of the scope of the audit makes the auditing practice itself a common mode function and is, therefore, a further source of system complexity. This is reinforced by the blurred distinction between auditing and consulting, which could easily impair public perceptions of auditor independence. In short, the consulting focus of business risk audits draw groups that previously belonged to the environment into the audit system thus making system interaction even more complex and delicate.

Another source of complexity follows from the expansion in the types of risk considered in the audit. Business risk audits now include analyses of political as well as social risks (see for instance Eilifsen et al. (2001) and Hayes et al. (2005)). Drawing the broader environment into the audit system is most likely a necessity in terms of the above mentioned going concern evaluations. However, since it is difficult to draw the boundary of the social and political environment, it becomes increasingly difficult for the auditor to establish which parts are relevant for the audit system. In addition, the social and political parts of the audit system largely interact independently of the audit firm and the client thereby further audit complexity. Treating the client as a complex organization, therefore, makes auditing equally complex.

Business risk audits are also susceptible to the kind of complexity that follows from misinterpretations of signals from the system. A lot of audit evidence[15] is now collected by means of benchmarking and other analytical procedures[16]. Benchmarking performance and accounting principles against industry best practice inevitably involves determining whether any deviation is within the normal and acceptable range. If so, the auditor will take a good deal of evidence from this. If not, additional audit work will be needed. The same goes for the materiality[17] judgments, where the auditor is supposed to establish the acceptable level of accumulated errors in the accounts. The more the findings from the audit need interpretation, the more complex the audit gets. In the Enron case for instance, Arthur Andersen considered an error of $51 million to be immaterial, and consequently not to be corrected in a year when the reported income was $105 million (Brody et al., 2003). Since business risk audits rely heavily on such subjective judgments and on benchmarking for additional evidence, it adds to system complexity. Business risk audits are therefore characterized by a move towards increased complexity in interaction and is therefore to be located in the right hand side of Perrow's matrix displayed in Figure 4.5.

Power (2003: 392) describes auditing practice as a loosely coupled self-regulatory system, whose components interact internally as well as with the economic, regulatory, and political environment. However, the Andersen case, where an audit failure in one Andersen office lead to the collapse of the entire firm as well as government intervention in the self-regulatory system, indicates that coupling in the auditing system may be a good deal tighter than believed earlier. The shift to business risk audits also tends to make the coupling somewhat tighter itself. There are two things causing this. First, as Eilifsen et al. (2001) note, most of the work in business risk audits is done after year-end. This narrows the time for the audit and thereby reduces the possible slack. Second, according to the new risk standards[18] the auditor is no

---

[15] Audit evidence is the information the auditor obtains in order to arrive at the conclusions on which the audit opinion is based.

[16] The analysis of ratios and trends and the following investigation into deviances is usually considered to be a cost effective audit technique.

[17] An error is material if it would affect the economic decisions of users of the financial statements. Immaterial errors detected by the auditor are not necessarily corrected.

[18] International Standards on Auditing 315, 330, and 500. The risk standards presuppose that risk management is undertaken and prescribe an audit strategy

longer allowed to disregard the internal control system and choose an alternative substantive testing strategy. With less alternative strategies possible the coupling in business risk audits becomes tighter.

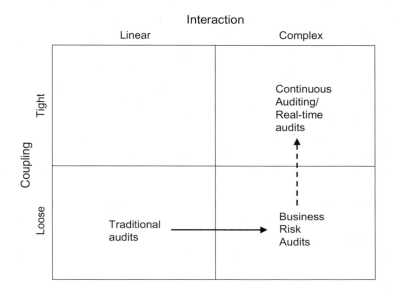

Figure 5.5   Auditing in the Interaction/Coupling Chart.

This does not necessarily mean that BRA has turned auditing into a tightly coupled system, and even if it had auditing does not have the life-threatening catastrophic potential of, for instance nuclear power production. However, the Andersen case clearly shows that audit failures can have serious personal and economic consequences[19]. The tightened the coupling in the auditing system combined with the increased complexity in auditing is, therefore, a problem that needs attention in the risk management of audit firms. Research nevertheless indicates that the partnership structure of audit firms makes strategic decision-making and, therefore, also strategic risk management very

---

based on evaluating and testing the strategic risk management controls that are implemented.

[19] In the Enron case shareholders lost $66.4 billion and 6,100 people lost their job. In the WorldCom case shareholders lost incredible $179.3 billion and 17,000 jobs were lost (Brooks, 2004: 88). In addition, the 85,000 employees of Arthur Andersen lost their jobs although many of them quickly found work in the audit firms that took over Andersen's clients.

difficult and slow (Greenwood et al., 1990, 2003). In other words, audit firms are typically poorly organized to deal with the increased risk following the transition of their main service.

In one of the more recent auditing fads, it has been suggested that there is much to be gained by turning auditing into "continuous auditing" or real-time auditing where the audit opinion is given simultaneously with or shortly after the occurrence of the event being audited (see for instance Kogan et al., 1999; CICA, 1999; Alles et al., 2002; Rezaee et al., 2002; Pushkin, 2003). Continuous auditing fundamentally changes the nature of the audit evidence. Evidence types that are based on a delay between the event and the audit, and/or require external comparison such as all types of confirmation and physical examination will disappear. This forces the auditor to rely on observation, analytical procedures and re-performance, types of evidence that have previously been considered relatively weak mainly because of the lack of objectivity. The disappearance of a time lag between the event and the audit gives no time for substituting audit procedures, which in turn makes the coupling in the audit system very tight. Since continuous audits are based on highly automated systems with many control parameters that are potentially interacting, it is very likely that these systems will also involve complex interaction. This means that continuous auditing is likely to be placed in the upper right box in Figure 5.5. If this is the case, continuous audits will also constitute highly risky audits.

Conclusion and Perspectives

The theory of risk in systems presented by Perrow (1984/1999) under the heading *normal accident theory* was specifically designed for analysis of risk in technological systems, where the distinction between the system and its environment is relative easy. Social systems, on the other hand, are seldom "stand-alone" but generally highly interconnected. If the theory is applied to social systems, the boundaries of the system must be expanded to include wider parts of the environment as suggested in the auditing system discussed above where clients and users of financial statements are included. The fact that the theory is flexible enough to allow this is probably one of the more important reasons that Weick (2004) still considers normal accident theory an up-to-date general framework for empirical analysis of the risk of any kind of organization.

This paper has analyzed the transition of auditing into what is known as "business risk audits". I have argued that auditing becomes more risky mainly because the object of the audit has been expanded from just being the annual accounts of the firm to include all of its interdependencies with the environment. Thereby a high degree of complexity in interaction is added to the auditing system, a complexity that increases risk. As such, the audit case is, therefore, well suited to explain the persistency and adequacy of Perrow's normal accident theory. It provides evidence that the bigger and more all embracing a system becomes, the more complex interaction also tends to get, which in turn increases risk. Since large scale social systems will almost always involve fairly complex interaction, normal accident theory is certain to provide insights about the risk that follows this complexity.

Complexity in systems is not necessarily unwanted as Perrow points out. It generally leads to more efficient production than linear systems. There is less slack in the form of overcapacity, more multifunction components and less tolerance of low-quality production. Furthermore, the unexpected interactions in complex systems leads to innovation, they amuse or simply provide more variety than the linear systems, thus making work more fun. So, complexity is not something that generally should be avoided but it needs to be managed properly. To manage the risk that comes with complexity in interaction a high degree of decentralization is generally needed. This is because failures will typically involve interaction between parts, units, or subsystems in unpredictable ways. Since unpredictable failures are impossible to control centrally, a high degree of decentralization is needed to deal with the risk that follows complexity. However, most audit firms are still highly centralized and are, therefore, not in a good position to manage the risks that are facing them as a consequence of the change in audit approaches. System failures will inevitably occur and the firms are not organized in a way that enables a quick and decisive response to these failures.

What should be of particular interest in risk analysis is the eventual catastrophic potential of systems where complex interaction is combined with tight coupling. In these cases complexity makes risk unpredictable and it therefore needs to be controlled by decentralized approaches, but at the same time the tight coupling requires a centrally designed control system to be able to react fast to the problems. Risk in complex systems with tight coupling is therefore very hard if not impossible to manage.

In addition to the common explanation that it was all due to a dysfunctional internal culture (Squires et al., 2003; Toffler, 2003; Wyatt, 2004), the fate of Andersen may well be seen as such an unpredictable systems failure in a relatively tightly coupled and complex system. Certainly, the Andersen culture was dysfunctional, but neither the culture nor the structure of Andersen was substantially different from that of the other big firms, except perhaps from a somewhat arrogant and eliteist self-understanding (Stevens, 1991: 13-24). What Perrow calls "normal accidents" are, therefore, bound to occur in the big audit firms from time to time. The many cases referred to in the introduction over the last five years seem to support this theory. Since such accidents also affect image and reputation, they are particularly damaging to an audit firm whose main service – the audit is based on public trust in its employees and partners. Audit firms therefore tend to think more and more in terms of reputational risk management. Because reputational risk management is "the risk management of everything" (Power, 2004) this only increases the perceived complexity of the system and the risks facing the organization. The consequence is an almost self-reinforced view of the world where more risk management gradually expands the boundary of a social system, which in turn becomes more risky and therefore subject to even more risk management. The audit case analyzed in this paper, therefore, describes the paradox of strategic risk management: It only makes sense when it is expanded to include the environment but when this is done, risk becomes too complex and unpredictable to be strategically managed. Perrow's great contribution to strategic systems analysis is to remind us that strategic risk management only makes sense to the extent it is decentralized. Regrettably, the audit case also indicates that this has not been well understood by the practitioners of risk management.

References

Alles M., Kogan A. and Vasarhelyi M. A. (2002). Feasibility and Economics of Continuous Assurance, *Auditing: A Journal of Practice and Theory*, 21 (1), 125-138.

Bell T., Marrs F., Solomon I. and Howard T. (1997). Auditing Organizations Through a Strategic Systems Lens. KPMG Peat Marwick LLP.

Bell T. and Solomon I. (2002). Cases in Strategic-Systems Auditing. KPMG LLP.

Brody R. G., Lowe D. J. and Pany K. (2003). Could $51 million be immaterial when Enron reports income of $105 million? *Accounting Horizons*, 17 (2), 153-160.

Brooks L. J. (2004). Business Ethics for Directors, Executives & Accountants. Third Edition. South-Western, Ohio.

CICA (1999). Continuous Auditing. Research Report. The Canadian Institute of Chartered Accountants.

Cushing B. E. and Loebbecke J. K. (1986). Comparison of Audit Methodologies of Large Audit firms. American Accounting Association.

Dirsmith M. W. and McAllister J. P. (1982). The Organic vs. the Mechanistic Audit. *Journal of Accounting, Auditing and Finance*, Spring, 214-228.

Eilifsen A., Knechel R. and Wallage P. (2001). Application of the Business Risk Audit Model: A Field Study. *Accounting Horizons*, 15 (3), 193-207.

Greenwood R. and Empson L. (2003). The Professional Partnership: Relic or Exemplary Form of Governance? *Organization Studies*, 24 (6), 909-933.

Greenwood R., Hinings C. R. and Brown J. (1990). 'P2-form' Strategic Management: Corporate Practices in Professional Partnerships. *Academy of Management Journal*, 33 (4), 725-755.

Hayes R., Dassen R., Schilder A. and Wallage P. (2005). Principles of Auditing: An Introduction to International Standards on Auditing. Second Edition. Pearson Education, Harlow.

Humphrey C. (1997). Debating Audit Expectations. In Sherer & Turley, editors. Current Issues in Auditing. Third Edition. Paul Chapman Publishing, London.

Jeppesen K. K. (1998). Reinventing auditing, redefining consulting and independence. *European Accounting Review*, 7 (3), 517-539.

Knechel W. R. (2005). The Business Risk Audit: Origins and Obstacles (and Opportunities?). Paper presented at the third EARNet Symposium, Amsterdam.

Kogan A., Sudit E. F. and Vasarhelyi M. A. (1999). Continuous Online Auditing: A Program of Research. *Journal of Information Systems*, 13 (2), 87-103.

Lemon W. M., Tatum K. W. and Turley W. S. (2000). Developments in the Audit Methodologies of Large Audit firms. ABG.

Perrow C. (1999). Normal Accidents. Living with High-Risk Technologies. Princeton University Press, Princeton, NJ (first published in 1984).

Power M. (1997). The Audit Society: Rituals of Verification. Oxford University Press, Oxford.

Power M. (2003). Auditing and the production of legitimacy. *Accounting, Organizations & Society*, 28 (4), 379-394.

Power M. (2004). The Risk Management of Everything: Rethinking the politics of uncertainty. Demos, London.

Pushkin A. B. (2003). Comprehensive continuous auditing: the strategic component. *Internal Auditing*, Jan/Feb, 26-34.

Rezaee Z., Sharbatoglie A., Elam R. and McMickle P. L. (2002). Continuous auditing: Building Automated Auditing Capability. *Auditing: A Journal of Practice and Theory*, 21 (1), 147-163.

Squires S. E., Smith C. J., McDougall L. and Yeack W. R. (2003). Inside Arthur Andersen: Shifting values, unexpected consequences. Prentice Hall, New Jersey.

Stevens M. (1991). The Big Six. Touchstone, New York.

Toffler B. L. (2003). Final accounting: Ambition, greed and the fall of Arthur Andersen. Random House, New York.

Weick K. E. (2004). Normal Accident Theory as Frame, Link and Provocation. *Organization & Environment*, 17 (1), 27-31.

Winograd B. N., Gerson J. G. and Berlin B. L. (2000). Audit Practices of PricewaterhouseCoopers. *Auditing: A Journal of Practice & Theory*, 19 (2), 175-182.

Wyatt A. R. (2004). Accounting Professionalism – They Just Don't Get It! *Accounting Horizons*, 18 (1), 45-53.

CHAPTER 6

Contemporary Enterprise-Wide Risk Management Frameworks: A Comparative Analysis in a Strategic Perspective

Per Henriksen and Thomas Uhlenfeldt

Enterprise-wide risk management frameworks have recently captured a central role in the evolution of the risk management field. In this article we introduce and discuss four contemporary frameworks in a strategic perspective. These frameworks (DeLoach EWRM, COSO ERM, and the standards AS/NZS 4360:2004 and FERMA) all claim to go beyond the traditional focus on operations and loss avoidance, and thus target all processes within the firm where risks can be created. They explicitly claim to establish a linkage between risk management and the strategy process. A logic point as strategy formation is one key source of risk.

However, a closer look reveals that the frameworks basically exclude strategy formation processes from the context. The strategic focus is limited to strategy implementation, the inclusion of "strategic risks", and to traditional technical-economical processes. The frameworks are not successful in creating an enhanced focus on the identification of new business and growth opportunities. They also fail in giving practitioners advice on the key challenge of "risk consolidation", i.e., the process where key risks are prioritised, selected, and communicated upwards effectively and appropriately to the key organisational decision makers.

Per Henriksen, Thomas Uhlenfeldt

Introduction
Risk Management in its modern holistic – or Enterprise-wide[20] – form, receives growing interest from business life. This has been documented in a number of surveys (Miccolis and Shah, 2000; Tillinghast-Towers-Perrin, 2002; Turpin, 2002; Viles and Easterbrook, 2003; Henriksen and Melander, 2005).

Developments within the Enterprise-wide Risk Management discipline have so far mainly been driven by management consultancies of Anglo-Saxon offspring – easily demonstrated by the fact that 4 of the 5 above citations relate to consultancies. Research-based work is limited, and mainly of Anglo-Saxon origin.

A Danish research project established at the Centre for Business Development and Management (CVL) at Copenhagen Business School under the title "Strategic Risk Management in a Danish Organisational Perspective"[21] seeks to counter-balance the consultancy and Anglo-Saxon dominance. The project has been established in cooperation with some of Denmark's largest corporations in order to develop an Enterprise-wide Risk Management concept, which shall assist Danish (and other Scandinavian) organisations in achieving a holistic perspective integrating "genuine" strategic business risks, and being applicable in a Scandinavian context.

An inevitable element within the research project is to take a closer look at some of the most important enterprise-wide risk management frameworks that have been introduced within the last few years. We therefore set off to do a compare and contrast analysis vis-à-vis four contemporary risk management frameworks on a set of determinants found to be of key importance (during our empirical work) in the Danish / Scandinavian corporate context. This article partly draws on results from the more comprehensive comparative analysis[22] by giving specific emphasis on one – in our opinion - key aspect. That is how the frameworks relate to the strategy process as a whole.

---

[20] We use the term Enterprise-wide only to underpin the holistic nature. It is a not a specific tribute to any specific writer within the Risk Management field. Other interchangeable terms could be organization-wide, organizational, enterprise (risk management)

[21] Information on the research project can be found at www.cvl.dk

[22] Uhlenfeldt and Henriksen (2006). Fire moderne helhedsorienterede risikostyrings-rammeværker: En sammenlignende analyse i strategisk, interessentorienteret og kulturelt perspektiv. (Four Contemporary Enterprise-wide Risk Management Frameworks – a comparative analysis in strategic, stakeholder-oriented and cultural perspective) – In press.

The article is structured as follows. The next section presents the four frameworks of choice, and draws a link to other potential frameworks or guidelines. This section also provides a brief description of the rather generic structure of the four frameworks. The following section considers our rationale of addressing the linkage to the strategy process and its key elements and discusses the meaning of "Enterprise-wide" or "holistic" in the context of the frameworks. The subsequent two sections compare and discuss how the frameworks individually deal with the strategy process, including the aspect of "opportunity". The final section concludes the article.

Before we begin, a word on the term *"framework"*. Two of the four "concepts" present themselves as frameworks, while the other two uses the term "standard". Although it may be debated whether "framework" and "standard" are interchangeable terms, we have found no reason to distinguish between them. We thus use the following definition to encompass both terms. *"A structure giving shape and support to something"* and *"a set of principles or ideas used as a basis for one's judgement"*[23]. We therefore see "enterprise risk management frameworks" (or standards) as generic frames and structures with the purpose of being supportive to risk-related decisions within the firm.

The Four Frameworks

While the US and other Anglo-Saxon countries are frontrunners in the development and implementation of risk management frameworks, there are few examples of Scandinavian organisations having implemented an enterprise-wide framework in its entirety. However, there are a growing number of organisations considering their future approach to risk management, including whether a framework should be adopted, and eventually – which framework. Judged from the Anglo-Saxon experience, it is more than likely that Scandinavian organisations will accelerate their implementation of formalised frameworks.

For such considerations, we find it of relevance to provide potential adopters with some advice prior to their decision. Since the COSO Enterprise Risk Management (ERM) framework was launched in October 2004, it has been heavily promoted by many proponents around the world. It has more or less been marketed as the point of reference in enterprise-wide risk management. But potential adopters

---

[23] As the Framework definition in Oxford Advanced Learner's Dictionary (1995). Fifth Edition.

should be aware that other frameworks exist, one of which may offer a more suitable solution to their specific organisational context. Since enterprise-wide also means a close linkage to strategy, potential adopters should also be aware that frameworks deal differently with strategy.

For the purpose of our compare and contrast analysis, we identified four contemporary frameworks, which have all obtained some level of penetration and acceptance. For a quick overview refer to Table 6.1.

Enterprise-Wide Risk Management – Strategies for linking risk and opportunity (EWRM)	*Risk Management Standard (FERMA)*	*Enterprise Risk Management – Integrated Framework (ERM – COSO 2)*	*Risk Management (AS/NZS 4360:2004)*
James W. DeLoach (2000)	The Institute of Risk Management (IRM), The Association of Insurance and Risk Managers (AIRMIC) and The National Forum for Risk Management in the Public Sector (ALARM) (2003)[24]	The Committee of Sponsoring Organizations of the Treadway Commission (2004)	Standards Australia & Standards New Zealand (2004)[25]
Labelled "DeLoach" in text. In References as: (DeLoach, 2000)	Labelled "FERMA" in text. In References as: (FERMA, 2003)	Labelled "COSO" in text. In References as: (COSO, 2004)	Labelled "AS/NZS" in text. In References as: (AS/NZS, 2004)

Table 6.1   The Four Frameworks

---

[24] Federation of European Risk Management Associations (FERMA) has translated the English version to the Danish "Standarden For Risikostyring" (2003). We recommend potential Danish adopters to refer to the original UK version, as the Danish version suffers from a number of misguiding translational errors.

[25] AZ/NZS 4360: 2004 may be most useful in the commented version. It is the version referred to in this article.

By choosing these 4 frameworks we have consequently left others uncommented. Among these are Young and Tippins (2001), Doherty (2000), and Lam (2003). Despite presenting headlines and titles such as "Organisational Risk Management", "Integrated Risk Management" and "Enterprise Risk Management", they either focus distinctly on financial risk management or take a fragmented perspective within the risk management field. They do not, in our opinion, provide a suitable enterprise-wide alternative. Another document by Waring and Glendon (1998) provides an early, but fairly premature attempt, to present a holistic model, but can be useful in other aspects since it performs a thorough review of various risk management tools. British Standard and ISO are also involved in this field, but focuses on narrow industrial issues. The ISO Guide 73 is an explanatory vocabulary and definition guide and does not provide any framework proposal.

The four frameworks in brief:

1. DeLoach's EWRM

"Enterprise-Wide Risk Management – Strategies for linking risk and opportunity" is a comprehensive document encompassing more than 300 pages including appendices. It comprises definitions, specific guidelines on risk identification, risk assessment, and various methods of risk control within the enterprise-wide context. The author, James W. DeLoach, was at the time of publication partner of Arthur Andersen in the United States. DeLoach also played a role in the formulation of the COSO ERM framework (see below).

2. COSO's ERM

The Committee of Sponsoring Organizations of the Treadway Commission (COSO) submitted their *"Enterprise Risk Management - Integrated Framework"* in autumn 2004. The COSO framework has been heavily promoted from many sides as the reference framework of Enterprise Risk Management. The document comprises two volumes. Volume I gives a 125 page presentation of framework structure, recommendations for key risk management activities, and guidelines for internal supportive initiatives. Volume II presents a long range of application and implementation techniques over 100 pages. The framework has been developed in cooperation with PriceWaterhouseCoopers (and James W. DeLoach). The framework is sometimes referred to as COSO 2, as it built upon COSO's *"Internal Control – Integrated Framework"* issued in 1992 (COSO, 1992).

3. FERMA (The UK Risk Management Standard)

The FERMA standard (published by the Federation of European Risk Management Associations) has been developed in cooperation between three UK-based risk management organisations, i.e., The Institute of Risk Management (IRM), The Association of Insurance and Risk Managers (AIRMIC), and The National Forum for Risk Management in the Public Sector (ALARM).

It is a compact document of only 15 pages presenting key elements of a framework as a generic guideline for Enterprise-wide risk management. It follows the risk terminology presented by ISO's (International Standard Organisation) "Guide 73 – Risk Management – Vocabulary – Guidelines for use in standards).

4. AS/NZS 4360:2004 (The Australian/New Zealand Risk Management Standard)

This standard is a joint product of the Australian and New Zealand standard organisations and builds on recommendations from a range of special-interest groups and public institutions. AS/NZS 4360:2004 is a revision of AS/NZS 4360:1999. The framework is available in two versions, the core standard it self (27 pages) and a 116 page commented handbook (HB 436, Risk Management Guidelines Companion to AS/NZS 4360:2004). The commented handbook includes in-depth commentaries and provides various application techniques.

Framework Structure and Components

A closer look at the four frameworks reveals identical structures for identification, assessment, and risk response. Despite individual differences in wording and terminology they basically draw on identical methodologies. In principle, they present close structural similarities as demonstrated in our 6-stage generic model below (Figure 6.1).

The four frameworks can, as indicated in Figure 6.1 and from the brief description of the 6 stages below, be seen as normative decision models developed to assist decision makers enhance the quality of their strategic, tactical, and operational decisions. Framework structure and content basically aligns to the classical rational decision models with their key components of objective setting, problem recognition, identification of alternative solutions, assessment of consequences, choice, implementation, and control (see for example Enderud (1976)).

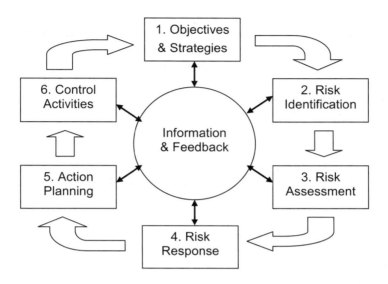

Adapted with inspiration from DeLoach

Figure 6.1   Generic 6-stage structure of the four frameworks

Stage 1: Objective Setting
Top management formulates and decides objectives and strategies for the organisation and the organisational risk management activities vis-à-vis corporate vision, mission and overall objectives.

Stage 2: Risk Identification
Identification of events with potential impact on the achievement of corporate objectives and successful implementation of strategies. Events can emanate from actions, decisions, or events within the internal or external environment. Identification techniques, such as macro economical analysis, industry assessments, scenario analysis, internal resource, and capability analysis are brought in action.

Stage 3: Risk Assessment
The level of uncertainty for identified events are assessed by means of a classical risk evaluation model, which considers the likelihood of occurrence of each event and links to the potential impact (consequence) on the fulfilment of corporate objectives.

Stage 4: Risk Response
Events are prioritised and response mechanisms determined. Response mechanisms are typically given labels such as risk avoidance, risk reduction, risk transfer, or risk acceptance.

Stage 5: Action Planning
Action plans are developed and implemented for each prioritised risk. Risk owners are appointed.

Stage 6: Control Activities
Control activities for each action plan are established in order to safeguard timely and correct execution of the decided response mechanism.

All four frameworks argue that the risk management process must not be viewed as a sequential one-off activity. The environment is dynamic; new risks emanate, and responses and controls previously decided upon may become obsolete or unfeasible. There is a need for effective information feedback mechanisms and continuous monitoring.

The Claim for Enterprise-Wideness

Beside the mentioned commonalities and generic nature of the basic framework structures, the four frameworks share another feature. They all claim to be holistic or enterprise-wide by nature and perspective, i.e., they seek to encompass all relevant risks faced by the organisation. Taking an enterprise-wide or holistic view provides the basis on which a framework can be attributed to the term "Enterprise Risk Management" and differentiate from the traditional narrow technical-economical risk management approach. Often the term "strategic" is being used, indicating a key difference to the traditional technical-economical risk management approach, through (as a minimum) the inclusion of "strategic risks" (see for example Slywotzky and Drzik (2005)). They seek to handle all types of risk (strategic, operational, compliance, financial, hazard, etc.) within a joint structure.

The basic argument behind enterprise-wideness is the intention to make risk management a cross-functional activity with the aim to *identify*, *evaluate*, and *manage* risks having a potential impact on the achievement of organisational objectives on all levels. It creates a platform for a mutual point of reference, a common language, and the sharing of risk knowledge across the organisational span of competences and functional areas. The frameworks thus seek to provide an overview of the combined organisational risk portfolio and their potential interrelatedness and thereby contribute to an effective, coordinated response in relation to the aggregated risk exposure. This contrasts to the traditional fragmented technical-economical approach, which has typically been conducted within separated functional silos, as pointed out by Aabo et al. (2005).

As the holistic approach seeks to establish a common point of reference and change risk management into a total organisation-wide approach related to all activities at strategic as well as tactical levels, one could expect the frameworks to target all the processes within the firm where risks can be created. That is, not being limited to a focus on the implementation of strategies, the inclusion of the so-called "strategic risks", and to operational-tactical processes, but actively seeking integration to organisational direction, i.e. to the strategy formation per se.

We find this an important point in the persistent claims for enterprise-wideness among the frameworks because business history presents a multitude of examples of "downside risks" being created within the objective setting and strategy formation processes (we shall return to the discussion of "upside risks" later). For the sake of our argument allow us to provide a few examples in support of our point:

- Swissair's collapse in 2001 stemmed from a series of strategic decisions in 1996–97. Left alone without being part of any major airline alliance, Swissair decided to build a global group on its own. The key strategy was to buy minority stakes in a number of mid-sized European carriers. The strategy became one of "escalating commitment" in financial terms, as stakes increased. In the turmoil after September 11th, Swissair ran short of cash and entered receivership in late October.

- The toy manufacturer and marketer LEGO is currently within a turnaround process. The need for a turnaround stems from a series of strategies, which proved to be rather tone-deaf to fundamental changes in buying behaviour. As the chairman points out in the Danish newspaper Berlingske Tidende (27th April 2005), Lego was caught in "delusion of its own historic success"[26], which made the organisation inattentive to radical market changes (although the information was present within the organisation).

- The fashion retailer Hennes & Mauritz has been losing market share to its key competitor ZARA for some time. Analysts attribute part of this development to differences in outsourcing strategies. H & M has long lead times built into their supply chains since a large part of production takes place in China. While this is cheaper, it also creates longer lead times, which may not be fast enough to meet a rapidly changing fashion market. ZARA mainly sources within Europe in smaller series – it is more expensive but also more agile[27].

Argenti (1976), Roxburgh (2003), and Bazerman and Watkins (2005) also provide a long list of examples that underpin our argument that risk management is not only relevant in the context of strategy implementation and operational activities. The core of our point is that for a Risk Management framework to be truly enterprise-wide, it must also seek to integrate the process of strategy formation.

This does not necessarily imply a need for identical approaches and methodologies throughout the entire risk spectrum. It is likely that risk management applied to objective setting and strategy formation should be handled by other methods and by other organisational players compared to risk management related to other processes. But a genuine holistic framework should comprise all relevant risk generating activities. Whether the four frameworks fulfil this ambition is discussed below.

Framework Linkage to the Strategy Process
We will address the issue by a closer look on two questions:

- To what extent do the frameworks provide linkage to organisational strategy processes, i.e., strategy formulation as well as strategy implementation?

---

[26] See (Lovallo and Kahnemann, 2003) for a broader discussion on "Delusions of Success"
[27] The H&M vs. ZARA sourcing strategies has been addressed in Danish newspaper Børsen recently (see Rosendahl, 29. September 2005 and 14. December 2005)

- How do the frameworks contribute to appropriate prioritisation and communication of key organisational risks to top management and board, i.e. to what extent is risk knowledge made part of the strategic decision context?

Linkage to Strategy Formation

All four frameworks explicitly claim to establish a linkage between risk management and organisational strategy processes. DeLoach addresses the relationship and the demand for consistency between strategy and risk management. He explicitly states:

> *"The risk strategy must be consistent with other firm strategies, regardless of whether it is formulated separately or integrated with existing business strategies. If the risk strategy is formulated after the business strategy is developed (which often is the case, as risk is often considered intuitively when formulating business strategy), then the business strategy needs to be confirmed and adjusted when risks are fully considered...(...) Therefore business and risk strategies should be developed concurrently – at least at a high level – so they are in sync with one another"* (p. 94).

According DeLoach, risk management should be integrated in the strategy process at an early stage and also make a link to strategy formation. The other 3 frameworks also address the need for linkage between risk management activities and strategic management. FERMA introduces its framework by the statement: *"Risk Management should be a continuous and developing process which runs throughout the organisation's strategy and the implementation of that strategy"* (p. 2). COSO recommends, that *"Enterprise risk management is applied in strategy setting, in which management considers risks relative to alternative strategies"* (p. 18) while AS/NZS is a bit more humble in stating: *"Risk management can be applied at many levels in an organization. It can be applied at a strategic level and at a tactical and operational level"* (p. 8).

The frameworks thus formally aim beyond strategy implementation and narrow technical-economical processes by an explicit focus on strategy formation. But close scrutiny of the documents provides a somewhat ambiguous picture of what this may imply in practise.

DeLoach is in practise not providing any direction to how risk management may be applied in strategy formation although he may presuppose the application of identical approaches. This is, however, not likely to be a realistic path considering the difference in focus, organisational players, and overall context. To provide DeLoach full justice, it should however be acknowledged that he touches upon the issue more than once. But, it is evident that EWRM in his view primarily is seen as an activity directed to bring coherence between already decided strategies and the implementation of these.

COSO explicitly links to "*strategy setting*" in wording. The headline "*Applied in Setting Strategy*" (p. 18 - refers to management's choice between alternative strategies - see also above) may lead the reader to expect some insight to be delivered. But COSO does not dig much deeper into the subject. In fact, COSO explicitly eliminates the link to objective setting within the framework of Enterprise-wide risk management, e.g., "*...but the particular objectives selected by management are not part of enterprise risk management*" (p. 26). Chapter 3 (Objective Setting, p. 35) delivers a few remarks regarding management's risk identification when choosing between strategy options (see also Chapter 3 in Volume II, Application Guide).

But the influence from the first COSO framework (*Internal Control – Integrated Framework*[28]) with its keen focuses on operations, reporting objectives, and regulatory compliance is evident. In reality, these three objective categories form the core of the 2004 framework – with the supplement of a new objective relating to the organisation's strategic objectives. However, this does not get much closer to the relation to "*strategy setting*".

Nor does FERMA enter deeper into the discussion. The only trace is an uncommented figure (p. 5) illustrating a (potential) impact by the risk management process on strategic objectives. AS/NZS keeps clear of the distinction between strategy formation and implementation, in line with the "humble" statement we addressed above. AS/NZS simply states the flexible nature of the risk management process and pinpoints that it "…..*should be applied when planning and making decisions about significant issues. For example, when considering changes in policy, introducing new strategies and procedures, managing projects, expending large amounts…….*" (p. 10). It is not providing the practitioner detailed advice but does on the other side not deliver over-optimistic promises.

---

[28] (COSO, 1992).

We find it a major caveat in the scope of the frameworks that they limit themselves to the identification, assessment, and management of risks of importance to the realisation of already defined objectives and strategies. In other words, they all take an execution focus. This is clearly an area of key relevance. But, despite explicit intentions to include strategy formation in risk management, the frameworks do not provide any answers or guidelines. Only DeLoach provides a bit of insight although his assistance is minimal. An alternative path is to leave the distinction out by providing a generic and consistent offer as done by AS/NZS. But considerations on context and methodology are left to the practitioners as with the other frameworks.

Linkage to Strategy Implementation

It follows, we believe, implicitly from the discussion above that the frameworks are primarily concerned with the relation to the successful attainment of already set objectives and with the implementation of related (and already decided) strategies and off course with risk management within operational-tactical areas.

However, if the frameworks are more concerned with strategy implementation than strategy formation, how do they then address the implementation issue? Do they provide useful and practical advice to the practitioners and do they actually seek to assist in the implementation processes?

DeLoach is quite explicit about the linkage to the implementation of strategies: *"Business strategies and policies are important because they provide a powerful context for risk management. For example, a thorough understanding of a firm's business objectives and strategy ...is very useful when articulating its desired risks..."* (pp. 91-92). He continues in his presentation of risk mapping techniques: *"The most effective risk mapping exercises begin with the firm's strategic objectives firmly in mind "* (p. 120). However, DeLoach is not providing any details on the practical alignment to the *"powerful context"*, not even in his risk assessment / risk mapping model (pp. 117-129). The methodology is thus for the practitioners to define, although a bit of advice may be found in the Diageo plc case (pp. 167 – 170).

COSO is also somewhat unclear in delivering practical support to strategy implementation but in its general comments it is clear. First, COSO defines ERM as *"..a process, ..., to provide reasonable assurance regarding the achievement of entity objectives"* (p. 16). Through ERM it also promises major advantages such as:

> *In sum, enterprise risk management helps an entity get to where it wants to go and avoid pitfalls and surprises along the way* (p. 16).

However, a few lines further down the same chapter (p. 21), COSO's strong link to compliance and reporting (Internal Control) becomes evident as it takes a firm priority on risks within the entity's control (incl. fraud and compliance to internal "codes of conduct") whereas the achievement of strategic objectives (through the implementation of strategies) takes a secondary role. It is, as stated, "*not always in the entity's control*".

COSO does not step back from assistance to strategy implementation. In fact, COSO makes explicit relations to the implementation of strategies. Chapter 4 (Event Identification, p. 41) puts up frameworks that can assist in the identification of internal and external events vis-à-vis the strategies. Chapter 5 (Risk Assessment, p. 49) also provides some insight. For example, by pointing out that time horizons for the risk assessment must correspond to the strategic horizon.

The very general and generic FERMA standard also links explicitly to the organisation's objectives and thus to strategy implementation, e.g., "*Risk management protects and adds value......through supporting the organisation's objectives....*" (p. 5) but does not suggest any practical advice for linkage or integration within the various process elements (for example, Risk Identification).

As the AS/NZS focus is influenced by the generic, flexible and widely adaptable nature of the framework (see also above), it would be likely to take a general stance on the issue. However, as AS/NZS explicitly define risk as "*The chance of something happening that will have an impact on objectives*" (see p. 3, for example), there is also a logical need to be more detailed. Chapter 4 "Establish the context" and provides some practical insights and methods, and describes the context formulation process:

> *The first step in establishing the context identifies the organizational objectives and the external and internal environment in which the objectives are pursued. The second step identifies the scope of the risk management activity and the main questions and issues of concern to the organization, and the relationship with the organization's strategy and business objectives.* (p. 30).

Chapter 5 ("Risk Identification") puts the identification process into a template, where organisational objectives form the backbone (p. 39). The frameworks thus become a bit more precise when it comes to assistance and advice vis-à-vis the application of risk management in strategy implementation. However, there are marked differences in the level of detail as COSO and AS/NZS clearly provide the most useful input to the practitioner.

Prioritizing and Communicating Key Risks

Practitioners dealing with enterprise-wide risk management within larger organisations frequently address a major challenge in the process. This challenge is linked to the strategy process. We label the challenge "risk consolidation"[29] by which we mean the process where the identified and quantified risks within various organisational levels are being integrated into a common framework, prioritised, selected, and communicated upwards effectively and appropriately to the key organisational decision makers. Effective and appropriate consolidation is a key factor in order to provide a useful basis for the purpose of good strategic decisions and efficient resource allocation. Hence, if the issue is of key interest to practitioners in risk management, one should also expect contemporary frameworks to deal with the issue.

The challenge is in our opinion generic but likely to be most relevant within the context of larger and globally oriented organisations with differentiated business areas and locations. Such organisations face deep complexity where differences in culture, expression of opinion, and valuations can lead to important differences in prioritisation and consequently on the consolidation process. These differences may lead to misjudgement in decisions in relation to the strategy process as well as operational-tactical decisions.

Large, complex organisations are at the same time, although it is not implicitly stated in the frameworks, the prime targets of the enterprise-wide risk management idea. So there are good arguments in favour for the frameworks to consider risk consolidation actively. It could however be argued with some right that the framework idea in itself produces some level of uniformity and a systematic approach in the capturing and selection of data. The frameworks also create a common language (a point argued in all four frameworks), which is a factor that

---

[29] With thanks for the inspiration to a key participants in our research network.

reduces the negative effect of inter-organisational differences in expression of opinion and valuations.

Besides the above considerations, none of the frameworks actually address the issue any deeper. It could have been expected that COSO – having its prime source within Internal Control and Auditing (the framework *"encompasses internal control"*, as stated p. 25) – had seen it as a key task. But, it is apparently not an integral part of the framework considerations. The same point applies to FERMA and AS/NZS. Only DeLoach touches upon the subject in the section *"Aggregate multiple risk measures"* (p. 199). However, his focus is not directed towards the "risk" of lack of uniformity in the process of handling risk data throughout the organisation (it appears to be assumed that uniformity is present). His key focus is on the "mathematical" aggregation and as DeLoach states: – *"aggregation is tough"*. He is probably right but that does not bring us any closer to an answer.

Risk in the Light of Opportunity

In the traditional technical-economical approach, risk management is typically linked to loss avoidance, i.e., to the management of downside risks. In some areas it is even explicitly accepted that risk can only be associated to negative outcomes, e.g., as underpinned by FERMA in relation to the "safety" field: *("......that consequences are only negative.")*. Within this specific context it is difficult to argue against the prevalence of downside risk.

However, by the emergence of enterprise-wide frameworks there is a growing attention directed toward the two-sided outcome nature of risk. The risk concept is closely related to uncertainty, i.e., the inability to make precise predictions for the occurrence of given events and their consequences. The risk notion stems from the Italian term *risicare*, which can be interpreted as *"be at stake"* or *"dare"*. The traditional meaning of the term thus implies two potential outcomes, i.e., loss and gain (see for example Bernstein (1996) for a thorough discussion on the risk notion).

Within this two-sided context, risk relates to the uncertainty of the outcome of a given event or action, resulting either in a potential loss or a potential gain for the organisation. In the context of risk management, risk can thus be defined as the combination of the likelihood of occurrence of a given event and its consequences. The broad definition of the concept of risk is frequently being emphasised among enterprise-wide frameworks. Such frameworks, including the four dealt with in this article, explicitly emphasise that risk management activities should not be limited to loss avoidance (or prevention) but should simultaneously take a focus on the identification of new business and growth opportunities. With a framework linkage to strategy this off course makes sense.

DeLoach repeatedly claims his framework's *"linkage to opportunity"*, e.g., that *"risk and opportunity go hand in hand"* (p. 46). He becomes a bit more detailed by stating *"the opportunities targeted by the firm's business model"* (p. 30). In his view, opportunities are being identified within the strategy process. Although DeLoach defines risk as: *"the distribution of possible outcomes in a firm's performance..."* (p. 271), he maintains a strict separation in his wording. Either we discuss "risk" in the negative downside meaning or we discuss "opportunity" in the positive upside meaning. The strict separation is underpinned by his use of the word *"severity"* in the risk mapping model (p. 119). Once again, there is a negative connotation as compared to the other frameworks using the more neutral *"impact"* (COSO and AS/NZS) or *"consequence"* (FERMA).

FERMA recognises the two-sided nature of risk, e.g., *"Risk Management is increasingly recognised as being concerned with both positive and negative aspects of risk. Therefore, this standard considers risk from both perspectives"* (p. 3). The FERMA framework provides some methods to identify and assess both sides but only relate to downside risk when it comes to risk response methodology. In practise, FERMA does not provide any considerations or guidelines to the handling of identified opportunities within their framework context.

COSO also recognises the two-sided nature but defines risk as negative outcomes *("risk is the possibility that an event will occur and adversely affect the achievement of objectives"* (p. 16)) and specifically uses the term "opportunity" when the discussion enters the "upside domain", e.g.. *"opportunity is the possibility that an event will occur and positively affect the..."* (p. 16). The COSO risk mapping model is in principle generic and may therefore not exclude a simultaneous focus on "upsides". But, the subject is not touched upon (not even in Volume II "Application Guide"). COSO escapes the dilemma by a smart move. They simply transfer opportunities to be dealt with in another context: *"opportunities are channelled back to management's strategy or objective setting process."* (p. 22). An effective quick-fix but one could have expected COSO with its high profile and detailed approach to provide the practitioner with some useful considerations.

Although all frameworks seek to position themselves as integrative of the opportunity aspect in their contexts, only AS/NZS deals actively with the issue. The AS/NZS provides detailed descriptions and guidelines to the handling and identification of opportunities within the framework context. As they state in their introduction: *"The program described here applies to the management of both potential gains and potential losses."* They take a consequent approach to the issue throughout the text. For example, the chapters on "Risk Analysis" and "Risk Treatment" present a thorough and specific guide to "opportunity" identification and its management.

We have often discussed this particular problem (i.e., the more or less "organic" focusing on the downside side of risk) with enterprise-wide risk management practitioners. Those practitioners who have reflected over the issue clearly admit the "uphill" nature of the integration of upside risks in their risk management activities despite all good intentions and efforts. The orientation is almost systematically directed towards downside risks.

What is a plausible cause to this apparent contradiction? We risk our necks by providing one hypothesis relating to the predominant strategy focus of the frameworks, i.e., their general exclusion of strategy formation within the risk management process. As we have demonstrated above the frameworks generally direct their (although they may claim otherwise) attention to facilitate strategy implementation and to assist the positive outcome from action plans. Action plans are not distant in terms of time perspective. On the contrary they are fairly close maybe only providing a time frame of one to two years. They will normally be followed by personal obligations vis-à-vis budgets, etc. for the manager being responsible and link to managerial reward systems. Within the organisational reality, where close (in the time perspective) objectives may even be rather stretched there will automatically be imbalance between "upside risk" and "downside risk" because the set, but close objectives do not represent the true centre line of the entire spectrum of outcomes.

This leads to an inherent and unavoidable mental focus on loss prevention. In other words "It is fine to deliver positive surprises but underperformance is a lot worse". An integrated focus on upside gains within the frameworks is in our opinion more than relevant but the discussion becomes irrelevant as long as frameworks in practise only orientate themselves toward strategy implementation. It becomes a play to the gallery because the implementation focus per definition excludes opportunity seeking. Opportunities are sought alongside strategy formation where processes are developed to seek new business and growth alternatives.

Conclusion

The four frameworks, DeLoach EWRM, COSO ERM, AS/NZS 4360:2004, and FERMA all contribute to the development of the risk management field in their attempt to establish an integrated platform. They actively seek to go beyond the traditional technical-economical risk management approach.

Each of the frameworks can assist organisations to establish a common point of reference for the management of risk across organisational functions and cultural barriers through a template of proven methodologies. A key benefit is the formulation of a common risk language, which can support an enhanced overview of the organisation's aggregated risk portfolio and the potential interdependency between risks. The framework idea thus promotes the sharing of relevant risk knowledge across organisational silos.

The attributes pinpointed above are, in our opinion, vital preconditions for the claim of enterprise-wideness. However, as risk management frameworks claim to be enterprise-wide, or holistic, one should also expect them to facilitate the integration of all relevant processes within a firm where key risks may be created. The key sources of risk include, as we have demonstrated by examples, the strategy process as a whole. A true enterprise-wide risk management framework should, in our opinion, therefore, consider risks emanating from strategy formation, strategy choice, and strategy implementation alongside risks emanating from day-to-day operational processes.

While some of the frameworks promote themselves, primarily DeLoach and COSO, they do not manage to integrate risks stemming from strategy formation in practise. At best, they relate to strategy implementation and to risks important for the attainment of corporate objectives. But, testing the robustness of strategic alternatives, which may be highly relevant in a risk perspective, is not a key scope.

The exclusion of strategy formation in the process scope has, in our opinion, another consequence related to the two-sided nature of risk. The contemporary frameworks pose a lot of attention to integrate opportunity seeking in the risk management process. However, the discussion becomes meaningless and artificial, and a bit of a consultant buzzword, as long as the creation of strategy is not dealt with as new growth and business opportunities are best sought alongside strategy formation. And again, although they claim otherwise the frameworks generally end up taking a downside risk orientation, which automatically lead to a focus on loss avoidance. The one exception in relation to opportunity seeking is the joint Australian and New Zealand framework because it takes a fairly generic stance to the strategy process, which in principle still allows for the inclusion of strategy formation and provides a consistent methodology vis-à-vis downside as well as upside risks.

We have also touched upon another key issue of concern to many risk management practitioners, i.e., the challenge of "risk consolidation". Risk consolidation relates to effective and appropriate prioritisation and communication of key risks within the organisation. Inadequate consolidation may negatively affect the platform for good strategic decisions and resource allocation and should, therefore, be dealt with (in the form of guidelines and potential approach) in the context of a true Enterprise-wide risk management framework.

Although these four contemporary and often adopted frameworks offer a number of benefits for the firm in terms of structure and the creation of a common organisational platform for enterprise-wide risk management, they also contain some shortcomings with respect to their strategy view. If integration of strategy formation and identification of opportunities is only a play for the gallery, we recommend leaving it out and instead concentrate focus on the downsides, which can affect given objectives and successful implementation of set strategies.

References

Aabo, T., Fraser, J. R. S. and Simkins, B. J. (2005). The Rise and Evolution of the Chief Risk Officer: Enterprise Risk Management at Hydro One. *Journal of Applied Corporate Finance*, 17(3), 18-31.

Argenti, J. (1976). *Corporate Collapse: The Causes and Symptoms.* McGraw-Hill, London.

AS/NZS (2004). *Risk Management 4360:2000 (HB 436 Risk Management Guidelines Companion to AS/NZS 4360:2004) - Retrievable at www.standards.com.au*

Bazerman, M. H. and Watkins, M. D. (2005). *Predictable Surprises. The disasters you should have seen coming, and how to prevent them.* Harvard Business School Publishing, Boston, MA.

Bernstein, P. L. (1996). *Against the Gods. The Remarkable Story of Risk.* Wiley, New York.

COSO (1992). *Internal Control - Integrated Framework.* COSO

(The Committee of Sponsoring Organizations of the Treadway Commission); www.coso.org - *Retrievable from* AICPA (American Institute of Certified Public Accountants) *at www.cpa2biz.com*

COSO (2004). *Enterprise Risk Management – Integrated Framework.*COSO (The Committee of Sponsoring Organizations of the Treadway Commission); www.coso.org - *Retrievable from* AICPA (American Institute of Certified Public Accountants) *at www.cpa2biz.com*

DeLoach, J. W. (2000). *Enterprise-wide Risk Management: Strategies for Linking Risk and Opportunity.* Financial Times Prentice Hall, London.

Doherty, N. A. (2000). *Integrated Risk Management – Techniques and strategies for managing corporate risk.* McGraw-Hill, New York.

Per Henriksen, Thomas Uhlenfeldt

Enderud, H. (1976). *Beslutninger i organisationer – i adfærdsteoretisk perspektiv*. Fremads Samfundsvidenskabelige Serie.

FERMA. (2003). *A Risk Management Standard.* Federation of European Risk Management Associations, Brussels, Belgium – *Retrievable at www.ferma-asso.org*

Henriksen, P. and Melander, P. (2005). Risikostyring i danske organisationer – fakta eller fiktion? En dansk survey-undersøgelse.

Økonomistyring & Informatik, 20 (5), 447 – 473.

Lam, J. (2003). *Enterprise Risk Management - from incentives to controls.* Wiley, New York.

Lovallo, D. and Kahnemann, D. (2003). Delusions of Success. How optimism Undermines Executives' Decisions. *Harvard Business Review*, July 2003, 56 – 63.

Miccolis, J. and Shah, S. (2000). Enterprise Risk Management. An Analytic Approach - *Retrievable from Towers-Perrin at http://www.towersperrin.com/tillinghast/publications*

Roxburgh, C. (2003). Hidden flaws in strategy. *The McKinsey Quarterly*, 2003(2).

Slywotzky, A.J. and Drzik, J. (2005). Countering the Biggest Risk of All. *Harvard Business Review*, April, 80 – 88.

Tillinghast-Towers-Perrin (2002). Enterprise Risk Management in the Insurance Industry - *Retrievable from Tillinghast - Towers Perrin at http://www.towersperrin.com/tillinghast/publications*

Turpin, M. (2002). Pan European Report - *Retrievable from Marsh, UK at http://www.marsh.co.uk/PanEuropeanReport.pdf*

Viles, D. and Easterbrook, G. (2003). *The Value Agenda* (Deloitte and Touche, Ed.) - *Retrievable from Deloitte and Touche Enterprise Risk Services at www.deloitte.com/ie/risk*

Waring, A. E. and Glendon, A. I. (1998). *Managing Risk.* International Thomson Business Press, London.

Young, P. C. and Tippins, S. C. (2001). *Managing Business Risk: An* organization-wide approach to risk management. AMACOM, New York.

CHAPTER 7

An Integrative Framework for Multinational Risk Management

Torben Juul Andersen

Multinational enterprises that operate across liberalized global markets are exposed to a variety of risk factors that should be monitored within an integrative strategic risk management framework incorporating conventional exposure measures, simulation techniques, and planned contingency responses.

Introduction
Increased liberalization has made it possible to sell goods and services overseas and acquire inputs in different parts of the world. Communication and information technologies have reduced the meaning of geographical distance and facilitate planning, coordination, manufacturing, sourcing, distribution, etc., across corporate entities dispersed throughout the globe. A globally networked organization can exploit factor cost advantages across corporate entities located in different national economies and access regional competencies. However, internationalization also enforces financial, economic, geo-political, man-made, and strategic risks that require active management of the associated corporate exposures. This article discusses different types of multinational risks and outlines the contours of an integrative framework to manage these exposures.

Exposures and Hedging
In finance, risk is typically measured as variability in returns. Another interpretation of risk relates to the adverse economic effects of various events as commonly adopted in insurance. A variation of the downside risk perspective considers failure to reach upside potentials as an important opportunity cost. Risk can also be conceived as the difference between expectations and realized outcomes thereby capturing risk as uncertainty. We may define a risk factor as a hazard

that can induce future events in the corporate environment with a potential to cause adverse economic effects. Hence, there is a chance that some identifiable scenario, caused by one or more risk factors, can occur and inflict direct economic losses or impose opportunity costs on the corporation.

Common risk factors relate to changes in financial market prices, e.g., textbooks on multinational financial management typically relate risk exposures to earnings effects associated with changes in future foreign exchange rates (Eiteman, Stonehill and Moffett, 2004; Shapiro, 2003). The currency exposures arise when there is a mismatch between foreign exchange rate denominated receivables and payables over time that make the value conversion into the currency of accounting uncertain. The field distinguishes between accounting exposures that translate currency denominated assets and liabilities in the financial statements and future cash flow effects of financial and commercial activities denominated in foreign currencies. Transaction exposures derive from contractual obligations denominated in foreign currencies and operating exposures relate to future effects on cash flows as changes in foreign exchange rates affect demand conditions, international price developments, etc. Together, transaction and operating exposures are referred to as economic exposures comprising all future cash flow implications deriving from changes in foreign exchange rates. Most registered transactions are relatively short-term in nature, such as booked trade transactions but could also include medium-term payments associated with debt obligations, etc. Operational exposures, on the other hand typically relate to estimates of future, not yet booked commercial activities.

Interest rate exposures arise when there is a mismatch between the re-pricing dates of assets and liabilities (Saunders and Cornett, 2003). A corporation may generate cash from its current operations and obtain additional financing through bank loans and securities issuance to fund different investments around the world. In these cases the expected timing of future cash flows and the rate bases associated with the funding instruments differ and create interest rate exposures. These interest rate gaps exist in all currencies in which the organization has engagements and gap analysis should be performed to determine the interest rate exposure in each of the currencies. Average maturity and duration measures provide the means to determine overall maturity mismatches and interest rate sensitivities. The duration of the corporate equity position is determined as the duration of assets minus the duration of liabilities and the effect on the market value of the equity position (ΔE) for a given change in interest rate levels (r) can be determined as $\Delta E = -(D_A - L/A \times D_L)/(1 + r) \times A \times \Delta r$ (Saunders and Cornett, 2003). Hence, duration analysis can comprise all material assets and liabilities on the corporate balance sheet as long as the future cash flows that characterize the assets and liabilities can be stipulated to determine their implied market values. In a multinational enterprise, equity duration gaps should be considered for each of the currency areas in which it has assets and liabilities. Hence, a simple way to assess the enterprise exposure is to aggregate the effects of duration gaps across the currencies at prevailing foreign exchange rates and compare the cumulative effects with net income and total equity to determine whether the exposure is reasonable.

Multinational corporations are exposed to different financial and market related risk factors caused by changes in foreign exchange rates, interest rate rates, securities prices, commodity prices, etc. However, there is a wide range of factors to consider beyond the fairly narrow scope of financial risks and we may use a systematic classification scheme to consider these risks (Simons, 2001). One risk classification separates the risks in general environmental risks, industry related risks, and company related risk (Miller and Waller, 2003). The idea is to first analyze general environmental conditions and then gradually narrow the scope to focus on more firm specific issues (Figure 7.1). Environmental risks comprise factors that characterize the physical context for global business operations and trends in the overall socio-economic system including influences from natural phenomena, man-made disasters, and terrorist events. Socio-economic developments comprise evolving political sentiments, macroeconomic conditions, regulatory intervention, etc. Industry related risks influence the competitive situation of the specific industrial context in which the corporation operates. This comprises elements that are peculiar to the industry, such as, changing customer needs, actions of close competitors, technological innovations, etc. Company specific risks relate to internal conditions prevailing within the organization itself as they are manifested through the way work is organized, people motivated, decisions made, actions controlled, and so forth, and include operational risk, documentation risk, and commercial risk. The more we move towards these types of risk, the more difficult it becomes to measure and quantify the associated exposures and the risks begin to look more like uncertainty.

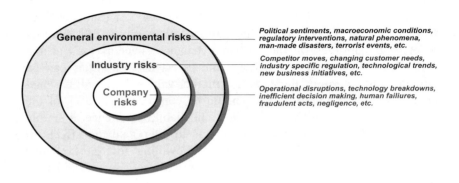

Figure 7.1 Risk Classification

Another method to assess the simultaneous impact of multiple risk factors is the value-at-risk (VaR) construct, which was developed to obtain a single measure for the aggregate exposure of many market related risks. VaR indicates the expected value outcome (loss) over a certain time period with a given probability (α). That is, there is a likelihood of α that the loss will exceed VaR over the time period. VaR can be determined on the basis of historical variance-covariance relationships between the market value of assets and liabilities. Variance-covariance relationships between the market values of different international assets and liabilities measured in the local currency comprise both interest rate fluctuations in the currency areas as well as changes in the foreign exchange rates. Hence, the local currency based risk measures incorporate both interest rate and currency risks as well as other price effects from changing business conditions, such as default risk, market liquidity, etc. The value outcomes of an invested portfolio or a corporate equity position can be determined according to this methodology and illustrates how an aggregate commercial risk exposure can be quantified and assessed.

Other exposures relate to the failure of human and technological interactions in and around organizations, including mistakes, fraud, computer breakdowns, etc. Country, sovereign, and political risk factors are related to default risk but constitute specific concerns associated with cross-border transactions as the corporation gets exposed to political, economic, and legal systems outside the home country. Casualty risks associated with accidents and the like are typically covered on the basis of comprehensive insurance policies. As long as the risk events are independent of each other, the underlying exposures are diversifiable across larger insurance portfolios and premiums can be determined probabilistically. Hence, large enterprises with substantial casualty exposures may self-insure these risks possibly through the establishment of captive insurance companies. If primary insurers or corporations have accumulated large exposures within similar types of insurance risk they may cede part of their exposures to global reinsurance companies and the reinsurance companies may in turn retrocede part of their exposures to other reinsurance companies to diversify the risk across the international insurance market. However, catastrophe risks represent extreme loss potentials and are not independent since losses are highly correlated within larger regions. Therefore, catastrophe exposures are usually ceded in the reinsurance market as facultative treaties covering specific risks. The reinsurance market typically deals in insurance layers where losses in excess of a deductible are covered up to a maximum amount, the exhaustion point.

The catastrophe events may relate to extreme natural phenomena and involuntary man-made disasters as well as terrorist incidents. A systematic assessment of these risks builds on preliminary analyses of the exposures. For example, reviews of historical loss records provide valuable background information to describe major hazards, such as, floods, windstorms, earthquakes, etc., and the direct economic impact can be determined in computerized simulations and scenario analyses. The resulting exposure profiles can be used to assess possible mitigation efforts and alternative risk-transfer and financing programs to cover residual exposures. The direct economic impact of disaster events may be determined from simulation models based on information about potential hazard intensities, listings of exposed economic assets, their vulnerability to the hazards, and the expected replacement cost of damaged assets (Andersen, 2005). Potential terrorist incidents are driven by human ingenuity that can be difficult to predict. However, loss profiles can be developed based on assumptions about possible scenarios and predictions from simulated outcome. Many strategic risks may employ comparable assessment techniques but are in some cases harder to identify, quantify, and assess. The handling of relatively rare disaster events is a major caveat in risk management because they are difficult to forecast. Exogenous shocks can encompass financial market collapse, international political crisis, military conflict, and civil unrest as well as major competitive moves and technology shifts. The multinational enterprise can only assume a certain level of risk retention across different risk categories and will employ various financial hedging, risk-transfer, and risk management techniques to cope with excessive exposures. The higher-level financial risks are relatively easy to cover in the derivatives markets. General casualty risks may be covered in multi-line insurance policies while higher layers hazard risks may be ceded in the reinsurance market on an excess-of-loss basis.

However, very firm specific exposures related to operational and strategic risk factors cannot be covered through conventional risk-transfer solutions. In this situation, management can consider natural hedges embedded in the structure of multinational assets. For example, in the case of long-term currency gaps, the associated economic exposures may be reduced by moving production and sales volume between major currency areas, e.g., so production takes place in undervalued currency areas and sales take place in overvalued currency areas. If a globally distributed manufacturing capacity represents operational switching flexibilities it might even be possible to exploit favourable currency trends by shifting production volume between currency areas during periods where the purchasing power parity is challenged (Kogut, 1985; Kogut and Kulatilaka, 1994). This constitutes real option structures shaped by corporate asset configurations and internal capabilities (Bowman and Hurry, 1993).

Arguments for Hedging

Corporations that ignore potential risk factors are hit harder when adverse events happen whereas uncertainty is vastly reduced if potential events are analyzed in advance (Bernstein, 1996). Institutions with high bankruptcy risk will not have sufficient funding available to pursue positive net present value projects and are, therefore, exposed to an under investment problem that reduces the economic potential of the corporation. Hence, a formal argument for hedging is that lower earnings variability reduces bankruptcy risk and thereby ensures availability of more favorably priced funding for sound investment propositions (Froot, Scharfstein and Stein, 1994). It is further argued that hedging should be pursued to stabilize essential stakeholder relationships, such as, employees, customers, and partners that engage in idiosyncratic relationships with the corporation (Miller, 1998). Hence, the corporation may have an interest not to jeopardize these relationships by having too high bankruptcy risk. Similarly, hedging and risk management efforts that reduce uncertainty encourage key stakeholders to make firm-specific relational investments that support persistent value creation and higher returns (Wang, Barney and Reuer, 2003).

Risk Management and Alternative Risk-Transfer

The risk management process formally starts with the identification of significant risk factors that have the potential to cause business disruption, create business opportunities, and affect the value of corporate assets and liabilities (Culp, 2002). The vulnerability to identified risk factors, e.g., market prices, socio-economic conditions, competition, disasters, terrorist acts, etc., are then analyzed. Assessments of potential value effects provide a basis to evaluate risk mitigation and risk-transfer solutions. Risk measures are used to monitor economic exposures and assess changes in the risk environment. Since environmental conditions change, the risk exposures are likely to change dynamically as well.

Financial and Market-Related Risks

Financial exposures can be covered by financial futures, options contracts, and various over-the-counter derivatives including forward rate agreements, currency and interest rate swaps, credit default swaps, etc. These instruments can limit future prices and shield against market volatility for intermediate time intervals within the accounting year and in some cases even longer. Hedging of financial risks can reduce unpleasant periodic fluctuations in corporate earnings but in dynamic business environments, corporations are exposed to other factors that are beyond the transparency of traded markets. Many risk factors are idiosyncratic to the corporation and its specific resource endowment and consequently cannot be covered through use of derivatives traded in the market but require other risk management approaches, including real options reasoning and responsive behaviors.

Casualty, Catastrophe, and Terrorism Risks

A central feature of catastrophe risk is that insurance premiums are very sensitive to large recent events that drain the capital reserves of major reinsurance companies. The insurance premiums also increase exponentially for higher risk layers because it is easier to predict higher frequency events in lower risk layers than infrequent events in higher risk layers (Pollner, 2001). Whereas these observations apply to all types of catastrophe risks, the uncertainty element is more pronounced in the case of natural hazards and terrorist incidents. Since terrorism is caused by willful human actions these events do not necessarily follow common patterns but may change character. This human influence is peculiar to terrorism risk and makes it more difficult to use historical event data for actuarial loss estimations. The focus of terrorist activities may converge toward more remote and less protected geographical regions where terrorists may target economic or symbolic facilities, which would predict a pattern of smaller more frequent events. Multinational enterprises are often exposed to such risks and need to take precautions against threats to overseas facilities and personnel. However, the geographic dispersion of productive assets, human resources, and business activities also helps diversify the exposures.

Competitive and Strategic Risks

Adopting a real options perspective can facilitate the identification of firm related flexibilities that increase the ability to avoid downside risk and exploit upside business potential. Flexible manufacturing facilities located across major currency areas arguably constitute one type of such options to switch production across cost effective locations in the multinational network. While derivative instruments provide opportunities to cover various market risks, real options allow the corporation to handle firm-specific economic and strategic exposures. The real options perspective was initially inspired by the idea of growth options created in conjunction with capital budgeting exercises. For example, investing to gain market knowledge and subsequently expand into them can create future growth options and investment in new business initiatives can also allow the corporation to enter new markets as conditions change. Structural flexibility and the ability to re-deploy corporate resources in the face changing competitive conditions are essential features of effective risk management (Andersen, 2006). Real options represent business opportunities that are distinct from financial options by their dependence on idiosyncratic resources in the corporation. The real option structures are bounded by flexibilities that allow the corporation to reposition in the real markets associated with input and output procurement (Figure 7.2).

The real options are shaped by corporate resources and capabilities, such as, assets, processes, and intellectual capital (Bowman and Hurry, 1993). Real option structures can, for example, provide opportunities to implement new technologies and procedures, offer new products and services, approach new customer segments, geographical markets, etc. A multinational enterprise has access to many diverse resources that provide a strong base for potential real option structures. The real options can be conceived as strategic opportunities that establish unique choices between alternative strategic paths and thereby allow the corporation to change market position. Corporate utilization of real options for risk management purposes depends on effective strategy processes where involvement and communication among key organizational decision makers can improve both options recognition and options exercise decisions.

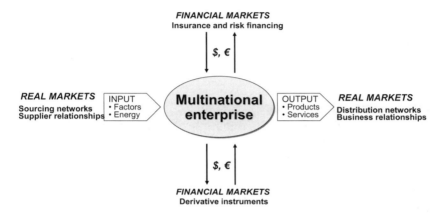

Figure 7.2   Financial and Real Markets

Integrative Risk Management

In many organizations, the diverse risks are handled by different corporate functions. However, this approach disregards possible interactions between risk factors. Instead the exposures of essential risks should be assessed in conjunction to determine how the corporation should manage the overall exposures through hedging, risk-transfer, and real option structures within a tolerable risk profile. This approach requires a comprehensive risk review of all business entities focusing on conditions permeating their environmental settings including competitive developments and organizational processes, operational infrastructure, human resources, etc. Such a focused review can help identify risk factors that have the potential to impose significant economic losses and inhibit the exploitation of business opportunities. Identification of essential risk factors creates awareness about important environmental conditions that can affect corporate performance and thereby constitutes a necessary condition for developing hedging schemes, risk-transfer arrangements, and orchestrated responsive actions. Some risk factors may not require immediate responses but are nonetheless brought to the attention of management for ongoing consideration. In many ways, this is exactly what is supposed to take place in a formal strategic management

139

process, which embraces risk assessment as an integral part of the environmental analyses. This is also consistent with a risk management process attempting to identify, monitor, and manage essential risk exposures (Figure 7.3).

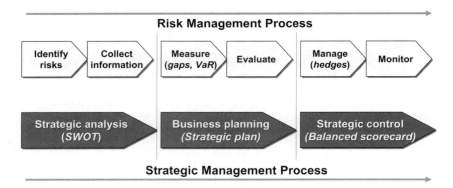

Figure 7.3 The Strategic Risk Management Process

The analytical exercises in a strategic planning process may result in the execution of actions aimed to bring the organization toward a superior strategic position and possibly consider contingency plans in response to uncontrollable exogenous events. While this can prove insufficient under extremely turbulent conditions, the analytical considerations will sensitize decision makers to uncertain conditions and the potential for unexpected events while increasing general risk awareness.

Conventional views on multinational corporate exposures primarily consider the impact from variations in foreign exchange markets and longer-term effects from changing macroeconomic conditions. In this context, it is important to consider interrelationships between financial and economic risk factors and not just assess short-term foreign exchange market risks in isolation. Over time changes in foreign exchange rates are related to moves in interest rate structures between currency areas as well as differences in demand conditions, default rates, and inflationary developments across national economies. Similarly, input supply, product demand, and competitive risk factors can be related to fluctuations in real exchange rates. In other words, different types of financial and economic risk exposures are often interrelated (Oxelheim and Wihlborg, 1987). Consequently, it is important as far as possible to consider interactions across the full range of risk factors that may affect future corporate performance including political, economic, competitive, and technological risks. The interrelatedness may also extend across other types of risk, such as, natural hazards, man-made disasters, and terrorist events as they affect macroeconomic and financial market variables. The major challenge is to consider all the relevant risk factors rather than adopting simple one-to-one mapping of risk exposures and hedging practices should consider the entire corporate exposure profile in an integrative manner.

The assessment of risk effects on future corporate cash flows is typically performed across different time horizons. Conventional analyses of financial market risks normally capture a near term perspective considering relatively short-term accounting exposures. However, the more uncertain and less quantifiable medium to longer-term exposures, including geopolitical and competitive risks as well as natural hazards and terrorist events can be equally, if not more important. Whereas this is generally recognized among corporate managers, it is rarely addressed in practice due to the ambiguity involved in the handling of hard-to-quantify risk exposures. The significance of medium and longer-term exposures of, say political, competitive, and technology risks is further accentuated by the changing nature of the external business environment where competitive disruptions are the order of the day in many industries. In many cases the true risk factors cannot even be known in advance and may arise without prior warning. Such factors can also include operational risks where corporations are faced with a number of internal vulnerabilities related to process quality, control systems, etc. From a risk management perspective both external and internal risk factors are important as well as unforeseeable events can occur and should be considered as hallmarks of effective strategic risk management preparedness.

Discussion

It is possible to use different derivative instruments to hedge and adjust financial and market related exposures but it might not always be a viable route. For example, it is not reasonable to use short-term interest rate futures and medium-term interest rate swaps to modify the duration gap of a corporate equity position, which reflects value effects on long-term assets and liabilities. In such cases, it is more appropriate to modify the maturity structure of the assets and liabilities themselves, i.e., if the duration gap is considered excessive it makes sense to reduce financial leverage and modify engagement in business projects with distant prospective revenue streams. In other words, traded derivative instruments are meaningful tools to modify short to medium-term financial exposures but if these exposures relate to longer-term economic risks, the corporation may need to adjust the underlying business and funding strategies. For example, in situations where a central foreign exchange rate seems to be developing in time cycles that exceed the maturities offered in the derivatives markets other hedging approaches are required to do the job.

Rapid-onset high-impact catastrophe risks such as natural disasters, man-made disasters, and terrorist events are difficult to describe with precision and the associated risk-transfer solutions challenge risk management practices. A multinational enterprise that has globally dispersed activities also has a degree of risk diversification because natural phenomena and terrorist actions rarely happen at the same time across geographical locations. Nonetheless, to the extent significant productive corporate resources are concentrated in exposed regions there is a need to mitigate and cover these exposures. Reasonably diversified risks may be covered through comprehensive global insurance policies or could be self-insured by the corporation. The large location specific exposures may be covered through facultative excess-of-loss reinsurance contracts or alternative risk-transfer instruments.

Other firm-specific exposures relate to operational and competitive risks that depend on corporate resources and the corporation's ability to deploy them in effective responsive actions. Hence, the identification of essential risks factors will differ from one organization to another partly because business portfolios rarely are perfectly comparable and because risk perceptions are influenced by knowledge imbedded in the individual organizations. The effective handling of emerging risks and unexpected competitive situations depends on an ability to sense environmental change and mobilize internal resources in appropriate and timely responses. In this context, the identification and creation of real options can be useful as the corporation considers alternative responsive actions although it is equally important to execute the strategic opportunities effectively (Andersen, 2000).

The foundation for effective strategic risk management lies in top management's imposition of an internal risk awareness and exposure monitoring culture. Corporate responsiveness requires a managerial mindset that is sensitive to environmental trends and openness to change that challenges prevailing mental models (Bettis and Prahalad, 1995). The corporation should maintain an organizational structure facilitating change and adaptive responses when significant environmental changes occur. Whereas the integrative perspective often is imposed on a formal planning and monitoring framework its execution also relies on complex informal processes that take place among corporate entities. Organizations that have the ability to coordinate work tasks across flexible networks of dispersed entities have a better chance to interpret information about environmental change and convert it into responsive actions. These networks can be supported by informal communication capabilities enhanced by advanced information technologies (Andersen and Foss, 2005).

Conclusion
General awareness about environmental risks sharpens an organization's ability to manage exposures more effectively. If management can engage key people in the organization to observe the changing environment and ponder about possible consequences, the higher the likelihood that the organization can construe effective responses on a timely basis. Engagement in formal risk assessment may provide a better understanding of corporate exposures and enhance general risk awareness. However, some risk factors cannot be known in advance such as new innovations, competitor moves, natural hazards, and man-made disasters. So, it is equally important to establish a corporate ability to sense and react to hitherto unknown threats and opportunities.

Torben Juul Andersen

References

Andersen, T. J. (2000). Real Options Analysis in Strategic Decision Making: An Applied Approach in a Dual Options Framework. *Journal of Applied Management Studies,* 9(2), 235-255.

Andersen, T. J. (2004). International Risk Transfer and Financing Solutions for Catastrophe Exposures. *Financial Market Trends*, 87, OECD, Paris, 89-121.

Andersen, T. J. (2005). Applications of Risk Financing Techniques to Manage Economic Exposures to Natural Hazards. Sustainable Development Department, Technical Papers Series, Inter-American Development Bank, Washington, D. C.

Andersen, T. J. (2006). *Global Derivatives: A Strategic Risk Management Perspective.* Pearson Education, Harlow, England.

Andersen, T. J. and Foss, N. J. (2005). Strategic opportunity and economic performance in multinational enterprises: The role and effects of information and communication technology. *Journal of International Management*, 11, 293-310.

Bernstein, P. L. (1996). *Against the Gods: The Remarkable Story of Risk.* Wiley, New York.

Bettis, R. and Prahalad, C. K. (1995). The Dominant Logic: Retrospective and Extension. *Strategic Management Journal*, 16, 5-14.

Bowman, E. H. and Hurry, D. (1993). Strategy Through the Options Lens: An Integrated View of Resource investments and the Incremental-Choice Process. *Academy of Management Review*, 18, 760-782.

Culp, C. L. (2002). *The ART of Risk Management.* Wiley, New York.

Eiteman, D. K., Stonehill, A. I., Moffett, M. H. (2004). *Multinational Business Finance.* Tenth Edition. Pearson Addison-Wesley, Boston.

Froot, K. A., Scharfstein, D. S. and Stein, J. C. (1994). A Framework for Risk Management. *Harvard Business Review*, 72(6), 91-102.

Kogut, B. (1985). Designing Global Strategies: Profiting from Operating Flexibility. *Sloan Management Review*, 27(4), 27-38.

Kogut, B. and Kulatilaka, N. (1994). Operating flexibility, global manufacturing, and Option Value of a Multinational Network. *Management Science*, 40, 123-138.

Miller, K. D. (1998). Economic Exposure and Integrated Risk Management. *Strategic Management Journal*, 19, 497-514.

Miller, K. D. and Waller, H. G. (2003). Scenarios, Real Options and Integrated Risk Management. *Long Range Planning*, 36, 93-107.

Oxelheim, L. and Wihlborg, C. G. (1987). *Macroeconomic Uncertainty: International Risks and Opportunities for the Corporation*. Wiley, Chichester, England.

Pollner, J. D. (2001). Managing Catastrophic Disaster Risks Using Alternative Risk Financing and Pooled Insurance Structures. The World Bank, Washington, D. C.

Saunders, A. and Cornett, M. M. (2003). *Financial Institutions Management: A Risk Management Approach*. Fourth Edition. McGraw-Hill Irwin, New York.

Shapiro, A. C. (2003). *Multinational Financial Management*. Seventh Edition. Wiley, New York.

Simons, R. (2000). *Performance Measurement & Control Systems for Implementing Strategy*. Prentice Hall, New Jersey.

Tang, C. Y. and Tikoo, S. (1999). Operational Flexibility and Market Valuation of Earnings. *Strategic Management Journal*, 20, 749-761.

Wang, H., Barney, J. B. and Reuer, J. J. (2003). Stimulating Firm-Specific Investment through Risk Management. *Long Range Planning*, 36, 49-59.

CHAPTER 8

Seeking Meaningful Country-Risk Information: A Wealth of Information, a Void in Understanding

Mikelle A. Calhoun

From governmental corruption to economic instability, foreign firms face a variety of unique risks when entering or operating in different countries. Country-risk analysis efforts by consultants, political interest groups and academics provide quite a variety of information, sometimes culminating in a rating per country. Such analysts, however, dissect risk into seemingly distinct categories of political risk, financial risk, economic risk, credit risk, corruption, and economic freedom. Thus, a question for managers and practitioners concerns the nature of the distinctions between ratings and the value of one rating versus another.

Introduction

Among scholars who have considered the issue of country risk, few have scrutinized the various approaches to and measures of such risk. Arguably, country-risk information is more useful if distinguished or dissected given differences between firms in their risk sensitivities (Bergner, 1982). Manufacturing firms will have more interest in political stability with related concerns about the level of risk of expropriation of capital investments. Service firms will be more interested in understanding the level of corruption in the host country labor pool. As a result of these differing needs, country-risk analysts have selected different foci for their analyses. Researchers, in reliance on these distinctions, have rendered opinions based on statistical analysis about certain aspects of risk and relationships between such risk and various management issues. Yet, others have raised various problems concerning country-risk-related ratings and criticism abounds (Barros and Souza, 1983; Erb, Harvey and Viskanta, 1996; Keefer and Knack, 1997; Cossett and Roy, 1991). Ultimately, it is unclear even with all the information how much we really know about country risk.

As explained in more detail below, the most significant problem of risk ratings is high correlation that traverses the distinctions one might attribute to differing labels used for risk measures. Individually, no single measure appears to contribute anything different than any other measure. Collectively, though, strength is found within the broader field of country-risk analysis. Explanations for the problem contain the seeds of a solution. Risk ratings aggregate information within and across critical dimensions to achieve one rating per country. Understanding the problem raises opportunities for new avenues of exploration, while suggesting the need for caution when making decisions based on country-risk-related information.

This chapter begins with a discussion of country risk analysis efforts and identification of specific risk measurement services. The second section of the chapter contains a discussion of the problems with risk analysis, measurement and understanding. The third section of the chapter contains suggestions for more accurate and appropriate methods of risk analysis. The final section of the chapter contains the conclusions and implications for practitioners and researchers.

Country-Risk Analysis

A Need to Understand Environmental Risk Differences

Country-risk analysis is essentially a sub-category and offshoot of international intelligence efforts. For centuries, spies and diplomats have investigated foreign governments and assessed their military capabilities, and then relayed this information to home-country officials for military strategic planning. In more recent times, as foreign direct investment (FDI) increased and the numbers of multinational corporations (MNCs) rose, world events such as the Iran crisis intervened and educated firms and investors of the importance of understanding environmental risk and how such risks differ across countries (Sassi and Dil, 1983).

Country-risk analysis has been defined as "the study of conditions, situations, and events that might impact favorably or unfavorably on conducting business or investing in [a] country" (Yavas, 1989:51, *citing* Merrill, 1982). Before the somewhat recent intense focus on country risk issues, academics had noted that the decisions of foreign investors often differed significantly from those of domestic investors (Hymer, 1960). Researchers realized that foreign firm faces greater overall uncertainty operating in an unfamiliar environment, and business opportunities abroad vary from those in the home market due to different economic, political, and cultural factors. This dilemma presented to the foreign investor has been described simply as "costs of doing business abroad" or as the "liability of foreignness." The local firm understands better the nature of the market and the impact there of local environmental elements. The foreign entrant may have technical advantages but seeks to compensate for a lack of knowledge by using comparative information to understand how the new environment may differ from its home country.

Foreign liability concerns often relate to a firm's ability to enforce its contract and property rights, should a dispute arise. When management is unsure of the firm's ability to protect property and predict outcomes of each transaction in a certain country, it perceives the risk of conducting business in that environment as being higher. Firms can control some transaction-related risks. For example, if corruption is a commonly accepted part of a society, increased monitoring of certain local employees may counter-act the increase in risk of employee theft or self-dealing. However, firms also want to anticipate country-risk events such as expropriation, war, and complete market failure in order to factor such events into their investment decisions. Finally, firms need information about environmental risks that might affect expatriates and local employees in this age of hostage taking.

Country-Risk Analysis is Born

The banking industry was the first to focus on country risk. By 1981, banks were already working with second or third generation country-risk models (Davis, 1981). Banks considered both internal and external information in their assessments. Research by *Euromoney* mentioned Union Bank of Switzerland, Canadian Bank, and Citibank, along with many smaller regional banks, as finding external analysis increasingly important as a check or even the only source of information on some countries (Anonymous, 1993: 369; see also Gordon, 1996). The concern of banks for unbiased, outside information led in 1983 to the creation of the Institute of International Finance, Inc. (IIF), which currently has over 320 members among commercial and investment banks, insurance companies, and investment management firms in more than 60 countries.[30] The IIF primarily serves the functions of analyzing risk in emerging markets, serving as a forum on key policy issues, and promoting collaboration between members.

As interest in country-risk analysis grew, measurement efforts encompassed different risk information and inputs. What began as one question developed into many questions concerning, for example, credit risk, insurance, economic and exchange rate risk, financial risk, political risk, and corruption. Motivation for the development of risk indices has varied. Consulting groups sell their information. More politically oriented groups promote their rating information in a manner consistent with their political interests or agendas. Investment or financial publications supplement their offerings with ratings information. Finally, some academics have proposed their own divergent approaches to risk analysis (Henisz, 2000; Simon, 1983).

Country-Risk Ratings
Country-risk measures and literature now have a diversity of focus. A review of existing measures reveals the use of different names suggesting different risk foci, different information sources, different scales, different weights of input, and different measurement approaches (qualitative versus quantitative). Some measures have a specific focus, others rely on a number of economic indicators, governmental issues, consultants' perceptions, or other indices from which to draw their opinions. No one approach is identical to another.[31]

The International Country Risk Guide (ICRG) has the most established risk ratings. Published monthly for over 20 years, the ICRG provides a rating for political risk, a rating for economic risk, and a rating for financial risk. Each rating is derived from various

---

[30] www.iif.com/.
[31] For example, the International Country Risk Guide's (ICRG's) Political Risk Index has 12 qualitative inputs; its Economic and Financial Risk Indices each have 5 quantitative inputs. The Heritage Foundation, with 4 quantitative and 6 qualitative components, analyzes everything from the fiscal burden of the government to the degree of black market activity to develop its Index of Economic Freedom. Euromoney's Country Risk Index has 4 qualitative and 5 quantitative inputs. The Institutional Investor bases its Country Credit Ratings on qualitative information obtained through one survey. Transparency International's Corruption Perceptions Index is based entirely on the ratings of other services, including the ICRG's ratings and information from Freedom House, which prepares its own risk-related index.

individual input ratings, including such items as corruption, which is a part of the political risk measure. The ICRG claims its ratings are "a standard against which other ratings can be measured," with use by "the IMF, World Bank, United Nations and many other international bodies."[32] Barron's, The Wall Street Journal and various academic institutions have relied upon ICRG's findings and have cited the strength of its measures.

Freedom House is perhaps the oldest risk analyst group. Founded over sixty years ago, its central concern has always been with threats to democracy and peace.[33] Freedom House began publishing its Freedom in the World Index in 1955. The index contains a rating for political rights and for civil rights for each country. Freedom House claims its information is widely used by policy-makers, journalists, and scholars, but specific information about users is lacking.

Heritage Foundation, established in 1972 in Washington D.C., is a conservative think tank. Heritage has a stated belief in "individual liberty, free enterprise, limited government, a strong national defense, and traditional American values."[34] Based on its ratings, Heritage has proposed the inclusion of certain countries in a global free trade association and suggested the ratings provide information that explains prosperity variance across nations.

Contrasted with these United States-based groups, the ten-year-old Transparency International (TI) organization, based in Berlin, claims to be "the world's leading, non-governmental organization fighting corruption."[35] TI widely publicizes its Corruption Perceptions Index, and authors of popular press business articles frequently cite TI's findings. However, certain business publications, such as *Euromoney* and *The Institutional Investor*, have developed their own country-risk related ratings as standard features in their periodicals.

The above list is not all-inclusive and in the last few years, there have been many new entrants into the field of country risk analysis. There have been new profit-driven entrants such as Global Insight, Inc. and PriceWaterhouse created its Opacity Index in an effort to gain prominence as experts in the field of country risk analysis. In addition, research efforts have led at least one academic, Professor Witold Henisz, to create a new political hazard measure (Henisz, 2000). Unfortunately, none of the analyst groups, new or established, provide

---

[32] http://www.icrgonline.com/.

[33] http://www.freedomhouse.org/aboutfh/index.htm.

[34] http://www.heritage.org/About/aboutHeritage.cfm.

[35] http://www.transparency.org/pressreleases_archive/2002/2002.08.28.cpi.en.html.

details concerning the relationship of their ratings to firm analysis behavior or concerning the value of their ratings over ratings by another group. Furthermore, under broad and specific risk labels, a variety of other risk analysis efforts range from collection of descriptive information to development of specific risk ratings. Thus, comparison-shopping for the perfect source of country risk information or of a risk measure, or even to determine the most useful approach to country risk measurement is difficult. There is a lot of information available, but little understanding of what information to use.

The Problem with Risk Ratings
Looking specifically at risk ratings, there is substantial variety in labeling of such measures, including: "corruption," "country risk," "freedom in the world," "economic freedom," "credit risk," "economic risk," "financial risk", and "political risk." Each risk measure draws from different information sources and has a different number and type of inputs. Risk-rating services use various scales and measures that draw from both quantitative and qualitative information to develop their results. The logic of analyzing different elements or aspects of country risk depending on the nature of a firm's transactions is consistent with a variety of management approaches and views. Firms with different types of transactions have different risk issues to consider (Bergner, 1982). However, the effort to dissect risk into various components or aspects of risk has been fraught with problems.

Distinctions among risk constructs and measures are neither conceptually clear nor empirically evident. A review of country-risk literature shows that full theoretical development and clarification of country-risk analysis is lacking. There is virtually no discussion across academic and popular press sources of the basis for distinctions between aspects of country risk. Indeed, comparison of definitions of different risks shows overlap and suggests confusion within the field. For example, one particularly problematic issue within the field of country risk involves the construct of political risk. Academics and others often use the terms political risk and corruption interchangeably, sometimes even including the concepts of transparency or "opacity," the latter being the label PriceWaterhouseCoopers has given its risk measure. In general, definitions of political risk reflect unclear boundaries between the central issue of the implications of political activity and economic matters and broader issues as explained by Sassi and Dil (1983: 2).

The term "political risk analysis" is something of a misnomer, for what we are really talking about is an assessment of the business environment, which includes analyses of the political and economic sectors, as well as operating conditions. Moreover, this is ultimately a dynamic rather than merely a reactive process, which evaluates business opportunities as well as risks. Occasionally this process is also referred to as "environmental analysis" or "business environment analysis," or even "country risk analysis."

In addition to definitional or construct development concerns are measurement or methodological problems regarding risk ratings. Prior analysis of variously labeled country-risk measures shows high correlation across ratings (Calhoun, 2005). This recent study analyzed nine differently labeled ratings from six different ratings services.[36] The number of countries rated by the indices increased every year. In 1999, analysis showed an overlap of 88 countries rated by the nine services. Correlations ranged from a low of 0.31 between ICRG's Financial Risk Index and ICRG's Corruption Index, to a high of 0.98 between *Euromoney's* Country Risk ratings and the Country Credit ratings of *The Institutional Investor*. The ICRG Financial Risk index and Freedom House's ratings are the most unique. Yet, even these indices have correlations over 0.5 with 4 or more other measures.

In addition to finding high correlations between risk ratings, a factor analysis was conducted on the nine different risk ratings. If ratings did capture information about distinctly different types of risk, a factor analysis would have evidenced that the various indices load as different factors. Yet, the finding of high correlation suggested the indices would instead load as a single factor, jointly explaining a greater degree of variance than any one index alone. As a second test, a factor analysis on the same data agrees with the correlations table and further supports a conclusion that there is no distinction between risk types. The factor analysis showed that a single factor explains 65 percent of the variance and the loading for each of the indices, ranging from a "low" of 0.64 to a "high" of 0.99. This single factor also passed the test for adequacy to explain the model. In a separate calculation,

---

[36] The ICRG provides four separate indices for analysis – primary indices covering political, economic and financial risk, and corruption, an element of political risk. Freedom House's Freedom in the World index is the fifth subject index. TI's Corruption Perceptions Index is the sixth index. The seventh index, first published in 1995, is Heritage Foundation's Index of Economic Freedom affiliated with The Wall Street Journal. The final two indices are both published at least annually in periodicals. Euromoney's Country Risk Ratings commenced in 1982 and The Institutional Investor's Country Credit Ratings, first presented in 1979, round out the list of nine indices.

the eigenvalue for one factor was determined to be 6.11, while the eigenvalue for two factors was less than 1, at 0.69. Thus, both the correlations test and the factor analysis confirm the measurement or methodological problem with risk ratings.

High correlations and the finding of a single factor for the differently labeled risk ratings undermine the presumption that country risk is subject to dissection into different types of risk. Further analysis of the input information of the same risk measures did not clarify the situation any further (Calhoun, 2005). Risk rating labels are just labels, distinctions between types of risk are illusory. Whether one is relying on a "political risk" measure or a "country risk" measure, the ratings will be essentially the same across countries. Research based on a measure of corruption does not really tell us anything specific about corruption. Instead of differentiated indices, country-risk ratings capture the same overall construct.

A final concern about country risk measures is the void between practitioners' approaches to understanding country risk and scholars' assumptions about the use and significance of risk ratings. Various researchers have relied upon one risk rating or another when looking for relationships between firm behavior such as foreign direct investment and country risk or an aspect thereof. However, risk ratings do not seem to be a significant source of information for firms and reliance on them is limited at best. Available information reflects that firms evaluate country risk using methods that range from highly complex econometric models to purely qualitative, judgmental approaches (Field, 1980; Miklos, 1983). Painter (1999: 52) reported risk information sources for Mobil Corporation include "outside consulting firms, [and] extensive use of internet and personal contacts" developed through internal and external networking.

Painter explained there are "scores of people throughout the company who may not be trained as economists but their jobs incorporate economic analysis". These employees were both sources and consumers of risk information. Meldrum (1998: 23) described the approach of Air Products & Chemicals to country-risk analysis as "based loosely on traditional country risk analysis" with "some fuzzy-logic" added to incorporate a longer-term perspective. Finally, Henderson and Cecil (1996: 48) suggested the FDI decisions of many firms are ill founded, based on "limited or misguided research." They concluded (1996: 48-49) that the most common shortcoming is an over-reliance on subjective rather than objective research – that is, general country reports and risk ratings produced by public intelligence sources and banks. Many companies [also] mistakenly assume that intelligence obtained from banks, lawyers, or their own executives is both comprehensive and factual.

In the midst of the various problems with country-risk analysis and divergent practitioner approaches, understanding country risk and its assessment is difficult at best. Research provides little or no guidance. Practitioners must rely on their own ad hoc, intuitive approaches to evaluation of country risk. The remainder of this chapter, however, provides some suggestions for new avenues of understanding, perhaps first applicable to researchers, and thereafter adapted to practitioners and managers.

Making Sense of Country Risk Information

While analysis of country risk assessment cannot confirm, and indeed undermines, the presumption of different aspects or types of risk, seeds of a solution may lie within the details of the problem itself. Aggregation of risk information to create one risk rating per country reduces the problem size, but results in the loss of information and in solution errors. For example, first, aggregation ignores differences in risk sensitivity across industries. Given that a firm's industry will affect the nature of its risk sensitivity, it is not much of a stretch to accept that risk will be disproportionately spread across industries by both type and amount due to transactional differences across industries. Second, aggregation ignores regional differences. Markets often reflect regional differences that are expected to influence types and amounts of risk in each market (Von der Mehden, 1983). Country risk information should be disaggregated to provide relevant information that is specific by industry and geographically by region or market.

In addition to consideration of both industry and regional variations concerning country risk, risk itself has at least two dimensions worthy of consideration. Assessing risk with one overall number overlooks the potential variation in amount of risk in terms of its pervasiveness and variation in terms of how consistently or how arbitrarily the issue of concern might be (Doh, Rodriguez, Uhlenbruck, Collins and Eden, 2003). As Doh et al. (2003) explained in their work on corruption the level of corruption raises one issue while the predictability or lack thereof in the form or arbitrariness raises another issue. If corruption is highly prevalent in a country, but arbitrary with bribes not demanded in every case, that presents one situation. Where bribes are not very prevalent in a country, but in certain situations are always demanded, that is another situation. The more arbitrary a risk is, the more unpredictable the costs of doing business. This distinction as created with respect to corruption suggests other ways to dissect risk. Risk can vary in terms of the likely significance of the risk. Using corruption again, it may be prevalent and arbitrary but the amounts sought in bribes may be low making this additional cost of doing business less of a concern. Each effort to dissect country risk should improve the information value of the risk information and allow for better understanding of different types of environmental risk.

Finally, it is interesting that despite the increasingly critical sentiment toward country-risk analysis, scholars have given little attention to exposing *and explaining* the deficiencies of this seemingly legitimate industry. The time is ripe for providing more guidance to international firms seeking to understand environmental variance between investment locations. Ultimately, this discussion suggests taking the analysis of country risk information to the next step by looking across industries and across firms to consider risk sensitivity differences. Then, the measurement of risk needs additional analysis to consider, at a minimum, levels of pervasiveness, arbitrariness, and significance of the risk. As a final consideration, current risk information may be lacking in distinction but the nature and degree of reliance upon such information appears to vary by firm and industry. Inevitably, both researchers and practitioners need to understand what information is being relied upon to make firm decision. Thus, in addition to gathering country-risk data in a way that provides more meaning information, firms and researchers should evaluate the information firms currently use in their decision-making.

Conclusions and Implications

Evidence of the importance of country risk is in firms' losses due to corruption, expropriation, war, and government intervention. IBM suffered financial and reputation consequences and was subjected to a SEC investigation when news broke of bribe payments by top executives to the national bank of Argentina. Coca-Cola suffered a four-month shutdown of production in Uzbekistan when its partnership with the son-in-law of the country's President became a liability due to a divorce. However, it is events like the Iran crisis, the invasion of Kuwait, and the Asian economic decline that have escalated interest in country risk over the last few decades. Firms must consider such risk in their international investment and management decisions, and researchers want to evaluate the relationship between country risk and firm behavior. Unfortunately, as reflected in this and prior work, the reliability of differentiated country-risk data and of research based thereon is questionable.

This chapter is intended to clarify the status of country-risk analysis and the value of country-risk information. The story of country risk analysis presumes that firms encounter different risks depending on the nature of their industry and resulting transactions. Thus, analysts have attempted to tailor country-risk information to fit different needs and motivations. Though logically conceived to account for variation in risk sensitivities and information concerns, risk measures labeled as capturing different types or elements of risk do not provide distinctly different results. Instead, aggregate risk measures are highly correlated and load as one factor. In the case of country risk, the similarity across aggregate indices arguably indicates strength in an underlying concept of country risk but weakness in the analytical efforts to distinguish between specific risk types.

Using the problem as a starting point for finding a solution and a more appropriate way to find meaningful country-risk information raises the issue of aggregation. Aggregation of risk information to the country level overlooks the influence of market and industry variance on risk factors. Further, use of a single rating for each type of risk ignores the dimensions of risk. This work supports dissection of country-risk analysis to find risk information that is both more complex and more meaningful.

A significant issue left undeveloped by this work concerns the intended audience of risk ratings and the types of information actually used by different groups including governments, industry, and academia. The diversity in audiences and their use of information may assist in explaining motivations underlying the risk-rating determinations. Risk categorization is an important element in the characterization of a country, the investment decisions of international firms, and academic analysis. For example, the International Finance Corporation and Overseas Private Investment Corporation provide support for organizations investing in emerging countries, which have high risk and high growth rates.[37] A government seeking foreign investors may benefit from having its country labeled as "emerging." A higher risk rating would support such a determination. Therefore, government and political interests may be more relevant to risk ratings than specific firm considerations.

---

[37] See http://www.ifc.org and http://www.opic.gov/

Mikelle A. Calhoun

Thus, a significant implication of this study pertains not to the measures but to the uses of such measures and the research based on them. Existing research that found a relationship between specific risk ratings and firm behavior may be flawed. Researchers need to be careful using risk ratings and should be sensitive to the fact that ratings likely were not created with them in mind. Instead, future research should focus more closely on the information firms are using to make their international management decisions.

This overview, analysis, and clarification of the field of country-risk measurement paves the way for future research in a number of directions that initially disaggregate country risk and then apply the newly found data to firm behavior issues. In addition, there are opportunities to explore what information is currently being used by firms. Finally, as new methods of gathering, organizing, and analyzing country risk information are adopted, practitioners and managers will obtain more meaningful information. This information should lend itself more readily to tailor the specific risk issues of concern to firms across different industries.

References

Anonymous (1993). The risk analysts analyzed. *Euromoney*, September, 369-370.

Barros, A. de S. C. and de Souza, A. (1983). Political Risk and the Risk of Political Blunder, in Rogers, J. (ed.) *Global Risk Assessment: Issues, Concepts and Applications*. Global Risk Assessments, Inc., Riverside, CA, 65-73.

Bergner, D. J. (1982). Political Risk Analysis: An Asset Now, Soon a "Must". *Public Relations Quarterly*, (Summer), 28–31.

Calhoun, Mikelle A. (2005). Challenging Distinctions: Illusions of Precision Assessing Risks of Doing Business in Host Countries in K. Mark Weaver (ed.), Proceedings of the Sixty-fifth Annual Meeting of the Academy of Management (CD).

Cosset, J. C. and Roy, J. (1991). The Determinants of Country Risk Ratings. *Journal of International Business Studies*, 22(1), 135-142.

Davis, R. R. (1981). Alternative techniques for country risk evaluation. *Business Economics*, 16(3), 34–41.

Doh, J. P., Rodriguez, P., Uhlenbruck, K., Collins, J. and Eden, L. (2003). Coping with Corruption in Foreign Markets. *Academy of Management Executive*, 17(3), 114-127.

Erb, C. B., Harvey, C. R. and Viskanta, T. E. (1996). Political Risk, Economic Risk, and Financial Risk. *Financial Analysts Journal*, November/December, 29-46.

Henisz, W. J. (2000). The Institutional Environment for Economic Growth. *Economics and Politics*, 12(1), 1-31.

Hymer, S. H. (1960/1976). The International Operations of National Firms: A Study of Direct Foreign Investment. *Doctoral Dissertation,* MIT Press, Cambridge, MA.

Keefer, P. and Knack, S. (1997). Why don't Poor Countries Catch Up? A Cross-National Test of an Institutional Explanation. *Economic Inquiry*, 35, 590-602.

Meldrum, D. H. (1998). Making a different at Air Products & Chemicals. *Business Economics,* July, 21–24.

Merrill, J. (1982). Country Risk Analysis. *Columbia Journal of World Business*, 17(1), 88-91.

Miklos, J. C. (1983). Country risk analysis at Wells Fargo Bank. *The World of Banking*, 2(6), 16–19.

Painter, D. H. (1999). The business economist at work: Mobil Corporation. *Business Economics*, April, 52–54.

Sassi, J. and Dil. S. (1983). The art of corporate crystal ball gazing: Political risk analysis experiences at Gulf Oil Corporation, in Rogers, J. (ed.) *Global risk assessment: Issues, concepts and applications*. Global Risk Assessments, Inc., Riverside, CA, 1-14.

Simon, J. D. (1983). Public News Sources and Monitoring of Political Risk, in Rogers, J. (ed.), *Global Risk Assessment: Issues, Concepts and Applications*. Global Risk Assessments, Inc., Riverside, CA, 99-114.

von der Mehden, F. R. (1983). Sub-National Issues in Political Risk Analysis', in Rogers, J. (ed.), *Global Risk Assessment: Issues, Concepts and Applications*. Global Risk Assessments, Inc., Riverside, CA, 55-63.

Yavas, B. F. (1989). An Exploratory Assessment of the Use of Generalizability Theory in Improving Country Risk Analysis. *The Mid-Atlantic Journal of Business*, 25(7), 51-61.

CHAPTER 9

Catastrophe Risk Analysis and Disaster Financing: A Country Perspective[38]

Torben Juul Andersen

The practical application of the risk concept developed in the financial industry, which has increasingly been adopted in the corporate sector can also be transposed to a country setting to deal with regional risk exposures. Risk management has progressed through an ability to quantify the risks and thereby allow institutions to measure, monitor, and manage their economic risk exposures. It also provides an opportunity to consider a range of essential risk exposures simultaneously, such as financial, casualty, and economic exposures. This approach is important as many risk factors are interrelated and therefore should be analyzed within an overall risk management framework.

Risk Management in a Country Setting

A country and the agents operating in it are exposed to a variety of risk factors including natural hazards, political risks, economic uncertainties, etc. Given the central role of government as administrator of public assets and political commitments, the associated economic exposures can be assessed similarly to those of an enterprise. Casualty risks that expose productive assets and resources are often caused by independent events, such as, accidents, fire, etc. Therefore, enterprises comprised of many exposed entities may want to self-insure these exposures because they can be diversified through risk aggregation. Conversely, small independent firms and households, that are unable to diversify these risks, would obtain cover in the

---

[38] Parts of this article are based on Andersen, T. J. (2004). Managing Economic Exposures of Natural Disasters: Analyzing Applications of Risk Financing Techniques. Special Report, Inter-American Development Bank, Washington, D.C.

primary insurance market. As a country's economic infrastructure is exposed to many independent risks, a government may be better served by self-insuring these exposures and maintain an actuarially determined financial reserve to cover future funding needs associated with the public commitments. However, the real challenge relates to the exposures of highly uncertain catastrophie events, such as natural catastrophes and mega-terrorism incidents. Natural catastrophes happen relatively infrequently but have a true potential to create economic havoc. These loss events cannot be diversified on a regional basis but the exposures can to some extent be covered in the global reinsurance market.

To deal with these challenges, a government could take steps to identify and survey the key risk factors that may affect the most important economic assets in the country. Assessments of possible impacts on economic infrastructure would allow the government to determine how exposures to certain risk factors may be reduced through active mitigation efforts and how residual risk exposures may be covered through various risk-transfer schemes in the global financial markets. If the vulnerability to natural catastrophes is reduced it would also lead to considerable reductions in insurance premiums. It might be possible to find new hedging solutions in the global capital markets but the associated premiums would be proportional to the potential losses they cover. Consequently, it is in a country's self-interest to mitigate the risks and reduce the economic vulnerability. The management of disaster risk exposures can be framed as a rational analytical risk management process, which first identifies the major hazards, outlines resulting risk exposures, evaluates opportunities for risk-transfer, and then arranges financial cover for residual risks (Figure 9.1). In the first step of the risk management process natural hazards that expose important economic assets in the country are identified. It is important to consider changing frequencies and patterns of the hazards in this analysis while remaining aware that the occurrences of catastrophe events are extremely volatile and hence difficult to predict. Based on the identification of major hazards, predicted hazard frequencies and intensities, vulnerability models are used to transpose the hazard analyses into probabilistic estimates of direct economic losses associated with possible catastrophe events. Improvements in construction, techniques, infrastructure, etc., may reduce the economic vulnerability but there is a trade-off between the needed up-front investments and the subsequent reconstruction savings. Risk mitigation efforts should be pursued as long as the future benefits exceed the up-front costs. Once there is a sense of the potential devastation that could affect economic assets, there is a need to determine which economic assets should be covered in a disaster situation. Based on the vulnerability analyses various insurance vehicles should be considered to cover specific risks and engage in up-front financing arrangements in view of the trade-offs between advance financing arrangements and ex post funding.

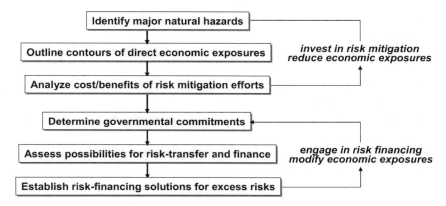

Figure 9.1   Catastrophe Risk Assessment

It seems reasonable to hedge against extreme catastrophe effects to shield essential long-term investment programs. It is argued that financial hedging should be pursued to such an extent that it ensures cash availability for all sound investment propositions (Froot, Sharfstein and Stein, 1994). Others argue that hedging should be pursued to the extent that it stabilizes relationships to all essential stakeholders (Miller, 1998). In a country context this means that hedging should be pursued to ensure that financial resources remain available to the country at reasonable costs and that global business relationships can be maintained even if the country is exposed to extreme natural catastrophes. A country that is adversely affected by natural catastrophes, and lacks the necessary response capabilities, could be faced with a significant credit downgrading that reduces access to international funding sources. Conversely, a country with a stable economic development path attracts foreign direct investment and facilitates needed long-term business partnerships including essential research and development ties.

Torben Juul Andersen

Adopting Formal Risk Analysis to Manage Exposures

A formal country risk management process starts with the identification of the significant risk factors that expose the economy. [39] Once the important risk factors are identified, the country's vulnerability to the various risks should be analyzed and the direct and indirect economic exposures measured to consider effective mitigation efforts. Risk measurement provides a basis for ongoing monitoring of the direct economic exposures in the context of environmental changes that may require responsive actions. The monitoring process helps determine excess exposures that should be covered through different risk-transfer arrangements. Hence, efforts to identify, measure, and monitor essential risk exposures provide a better decision framework for investment that can furnish economic growth. In practice the application of the risk management process builds on a systematic analysis of all significant risk exposures. Preliminary analyses of loss records provide background information to pinpoint major hazards, e.g., flood, windstorm, earthquake, drought, etc. Next the economic impact of the identified hazards can be determined from computerized model simulations or simpler scenario analyses. The risk exposure profile determined by model simulations can provide a basis for structuring relevant risk-transfer and financing programs that secure availability of funds for post-disaster reconstruction. By reinstating exposed productive assets effectively after major disasters have occurred, the economic infrastructure may in fact be improved and thereby have positive indirect economic spill-over effects.

The direct economic impact of natural hazards can be determined by use of relatively advanced computer based simulation models that stipulate (1) likely hazard intensities, (2) economic assets exposed to the hazards, (3) the vulnerability of the exposed assets, and (4) the replacement cost of the damaged assets (Lester and Gurenko, 2003). The simulations incorporate hazard occurrence parameters that identify the intensity of events and the probabilities of their occurrence derived from statistical distributions of historical events data. A stochastic set of hazard events determined by relevant occurrence parameters can be derived from historical observations of the hazards. Given the environmental characteristics of a country or geographical region, the intensity of the hazard events can then be simulated at different

---

[39] Direct economic exposures relate to the replacement cost of affected assets while indirect economic exposures relate to subsequent effects on economic activity in general.

locations where site conditions may amplify or reduce the impact of the hazard.

The magnitude of economic exposures to natural hazards can be derived from data sources that list public infrastructure. The size of the direct economic exposures, i.e., the capital loss or value at risk, can be found by multiplying the asset inventory list with the average cost of each asset type. Given the simulated intensities of the stochastic set of hazard events, the model can quantify the potential damages that are inflicted on different asset types across various sites as a function of the relative quality of the assets. The quality of productive assets can be determined by a classification of vulnerability, expressed in a vulnerability ratio that takes a variety of factors into consideration, such as, building material, construction type, usage, size, and age. The hazard intensity in combination with the vulnerability of the exposed structure determines the degree of damage inflicted by the event. The economic damage is measured as the ratio of repair cost over total replacement cost for the structure at different hazard intensities expressed in the damage ratio, technically determined as the product between the vulnerability ratio and the hazard intensity of the natural events. Total losses are derived from the damage ratio converted into a dollar amount by multiplying with the value at risk for the asset type. The expected losses can be found by considering the probability of the hazard events against the total losses associated with the events. This can be done for all the exposed asset classes at each site and aggregated into regional and country level aggregates as needed.

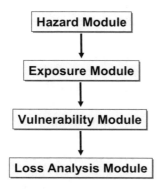

Figure 9.2   A Catastrophe Risk Simulation Model

Hence, the calculation of economic exposures is typically done in sequential modules: The *hazard module* determines the potential intensity of different hazards at exposed sites in the country, the *exposure module* outlines the exposed economic assets at these sites and determine the value at risk, the *vulnerability module* determines the damage ratio ascribed to asset classes of different quality, and the *loss analysis module* calculates the total direct economic losses of the simulated hazard events (Figure 9.2).

The calculation of the direct economic exposure, the expected loss (*EL*), can be formalized as follows:

$$EL = p * v * h * ICL$$

p = probability of the hazard event
v = vulnerability factor of capital asset
h = hazard intensity factor
$d = v * h$ = damage ratio
ICL = insured capital loss or value at risk

The exposed economic assets may fall within different categories. The vulnerability of public assets such as educational institutions including schools and colleges, medical facilities, hospitals, and health centers, and infrastructure, such as, roads, bridges, airports, harbors, etc., obviously constitute important societal and government concerns. Commercial and private assets may include industrial compounds, business facilities, residential dwellings, etc. A key objective in the risk assessments is to quantify the economic exposures of specific regions and the country as a whole.

   The model simulations typically develop a number of measures for use in ongoing risk exposure assessments: (1) the *average annual loss* (AAL) - the expected loss per year measured over an extended period of time, e.g., calculated as the sum of the products between all the event losses and the associated event probabilities, (2) the *probable maximum loss* (PML) - the loss severity expressed in pecuniary terms or as a percentage of the value at risk. Event losses can be considerably higher than PML but it provides a comparative number of the risk exposure[40], (3) the *loss cost* - the part of the insurance premium that

---

[40] PML is not universally defined but is often determined as the largest likely loss, e.g., corresponding to a 150-year return period, which refers to a hazard impact that

pays for the expected reconstruction of damaged assets and corresponds to the *pure premium* charged by an insurance company excluding administration, underwriting, and capital returns. Other outputs from the model simulations include two types of *loss exceeding probability curves*, i.e., cumulative distributions indicating the probability that losses from a catastrophe event will exceed a certain level: (1) the *Aggregate Exceeding Probability* (AEP) curve shows the probability that aggregate losses from all hazard events in a year will exceed a certain amount (Figure 9.3), and (2) the *Occurrence Exceeding Probability* (OEP) shows the annual probability that the losses of the single largest hazard event will exceed a certain amount.

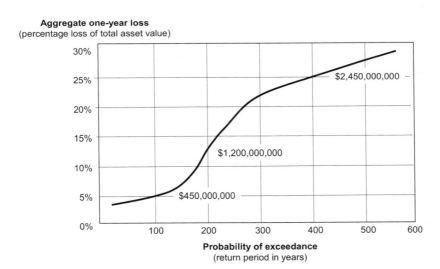

Figure 9.3 The Aggregate Exceeding Probability Curve (AEP) - Example

Since the use of catastrophe simulation models are rather technically complex, they are often performed by specialized consultancies and as a consequence may also be rather costly. However, there are alternative and cheaper ways to stipulate loss expectancy relationships, for example, based on historical loss records maintained by major reinsurance companies (Freeman et al., 2002). Once the expected loss profiles are stipulated the discussion of their significance to the

---

occurs with an annual likelihood of $1/150 = 0.67$ %. This definition may also differ across different types of hazards.

national economy arises to determine whether the loss estimates represent significant economic exposures? As an example, if the aggregate exceeding probability curve (AEP) indicates a 1% likelihood of a $450 million loss from catastrophes in a single year (a 100-year event), should that exposure be insured or could it be partially retained? The answer is subjective to some degree and depends on what is deemed politically acceptable. It can be argued that the government should try to shield the country's long-term investment programs from extraordinary catastrophe losses, in which case the measure of reasonable exposure should be determined in relation to the size of the approved capital budget.

Once it has been determined what constitutes a reasonable risk profile given the natural hazards that expose key economic assets in the country, the next task is to set up appropriate risk-transfer and financing arrangements. This entails an analysis of the costs associated with various ways to transfer and finance excessive risk exposures while assessing applications of different risk management vehicles. Establishing the ideal risk-transfer programs is not a clear-cut task and will entail tradeoffs between the level of risk cover and the cost associated with alternative insurance and credit arrangements.

The entire risk management process should be conceived as dynamic and ongoing. Since the environmental conditions continue to change, the profile of the economic exposure to catastrophe risks should be updated to reflect changes in climatic patterns, economic infrastructure, financial prices, etc. The ongoing efforts to monitor the changing contours of the risk exposure should also entail continuous evaluations of alternative risk-transfer solutions and adjustments to the coverage structure to take advantage of opportunities in the international financial markets. The dynamic character of the risk management process implies that the identification of significant risk factors is an ongoing exercise (Figure 9.4).

Simple environmental awareness or use of more advanced computerized simulation a models can help assess the changing profile of the economic risk exposure nd support the reassessment of the frequency of risk events and their economic impacts. It also provides the risk managers with an ability to evaluate the potential advantages of different risk mitigation, prevention, and preparedness efforts and thereby provide the underpinnings for more effective risk management decisions.

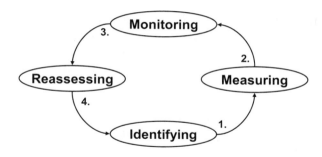

Figure 9.4   The Dynamic Risk Management Process [41]

The ongoing monitoring of the country's overall catastrophe risk profile provides the means to assess aggregate effects of identified catastrophe risks. This makes it possible to determine whether the country is moving towards an excessive level of risk and identify needs to modify existing risk-transfer arrangements. By monitoring and maintaining risk exposures within acceptable limits, the government can protect essential investment programs from disruptions to the benefit of long-term economic growth. By establishing reasonable risk-transfer arrangements, the government can also secure funds for reconstruction of key economic infrastructure after disasters and avoid time consuming and potentially excruciating negotiations to obtain funding after major disasters.

Insurance and Other Risk-Transfer Arrangements

Primary insurance companies insure homes, factories, inventories, crops, etc., in comprehensive policies that usually include some cover for catastrophe exposures[42]. Since the bases of these exposures represent independent event risks they can normally be diversified across large insurance pools and losses can be determined actuarially. However, excess risk exposures to natural hazards where events are regionally dependent may be ceded to reinsurance companies on a proportional basis so exposures are diversified across the global insurance community. The insurance companies use their reserves to cover extreme claims as is the case in the aftermath of a natural disaster. After major events the affected insurance companies increase

---

[41] Adapted from Culp, C. L. (2002). The ART of Risk Management. Wiley, New York.
[42] In regions that are highly exposed to natural catastrophes these exposures could, however, be explicitly excluded in the insurance policies.

the insurance premiums to rebuild their reserve positions. Some of the weakest insurance companies may even go bankrupt, which will reduce the capacity for catastrophe insurance. Consequently, prices for catastrophe insurance are highly cyclical and influenced by the occurrence of major disasters.

Large unbalanced risk exposures, such as catastrophe risks, are typically ceded in the reinsurance and capital markets as facultative non-proportional treaties. Facultative treaties provide cover for individual risk factors, e.g., flood, windstorm, earthquake, etc. A non-proportional treaty normally defines a deductible, net retention or *attachment point*, up to which the ceding insurer will cover all losses. The reinsurer is then committed to cover losses in excess of the deductible up to a certain amount referred to as the *exhaustion point*. Coverage within the attachment and exhaustion points is commonly referred to as a *layer* (Figure 9.5).

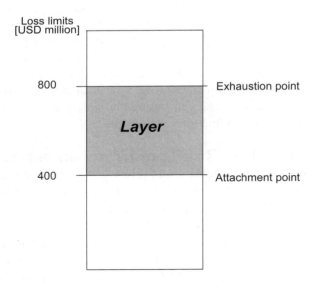

Figure 9.5 Reinsurance Layers

The cost of reinsurance coverage is sometimes indicated by the rate-on-line (ROL) derived as the premium divided by the covered insurance limit (e.g. Froot, 1999; Guy Carpenter, 2000):

$$ROL = Premium/Cover\ limit$$

The catastrophe insurance cover can be organized within different layer structures where a ceded risk exposure may cover a portion of the total loss between the attachment and exhaustion points (Figure 9.6).

The risk transfers can be structured in different ways, e.g., as *catastrophe bonds* or as *catastrophe risk swaps*, whereby the risk exposures can be placed with investors in the capital market and distributed between insurance professionals. These approaches constitute ways to extend and facilitate risk-transfer of different types of catastrophe risk exposures. Since the private insurance market may be unable to provide cost effective cover for catastrophe risks after major events other methods may be required, possibly on an interim basis, to make insurance protection available to the public for example through public insurance pools. This presumes an appropriate balance between the government intervention and commercial insurance involvement. It is argued that governments should be willing to cover a part of the uninsurable risk exposures as the *insurer of-last-resort*. Government debt supposedly has no default risk within the country, so the government can, at least theoretically issue risk-free local currency denominated debt instruments and thereby obtain funding for excessive catastrophe losses at the lowest possible costs. Government supported insurance schemes arguably have better access to risk capital compared to commercial counterparts although most governments also are subjected to financial constraints in practice (Freeman and Martin, 2002).

There are also potential downsides associated with excessive government guarantees for catastrophe risk exposures, because it can too encourage aggressive behaviors among commercial insurers to the detriment of the solvency of the domestic insurance industry (Bohn and Hall, 1999). The government could intervene more indirectly by supporting primary insurers in the country, e.g., through the issuance of catastrophe call options that cover losses on an excess-of-loss basis (Cummins et al., 1999). Under this structure, the insurance companies would have to pay an up-front option premium to the government as compensation for the expected future payouts under the contract. The option structure could extend the insurance capacity in the market and yet limit direct government involvement in claims distributions after major natural disasters.

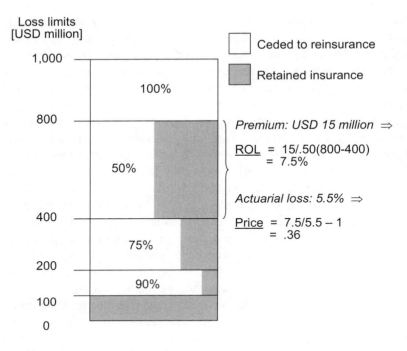

Figure 9.6 Layered Reinsurance Program - Example

Pooled Insurance Programs

The underlying rationale of insurance schemes derives from the ability to diversify the risk exposures and spread the implied loss claims across a large number of constituents. In the case of independent risk events, regional insurance portfolios may provide sufficient diversification and establish an actuarial base to determine appropriate insurance premiums. In the case of catastrophes that represent a series of highly dependent event risks at the regional level may be diversified on an international scale as international reinsurance companies spread different catastrophe risk exposures across the global reinsurance industry through various retrocession arrangements. Since insurance may be a relatively expensive way to provide full cover in a high exposure country, excess-of-loss catastrophe insurance contracts may be used to shield the government finances from the brunt of losses associated with major catastrophe events. Hence, a government may want to establish coverage through some form of pooled insurance program funded through tax increases and new debt issuance complemented by excess-of-loss insurance treaties to cover higher-layer risk exposures (Figure 9.7).

It may be possible to cover a certain part of the lower risk layers through insurance contracts with primary insurance companies in the local market. Higher risk layers that exceed the local market capacity could be ceded to global reinsurance companies. In some cases government backed catastrophe bonds might represent an alternative way of placing risk in the capital market. The highest risk layers are often too expensive and go beyond general market capacity. Therefore, various credit arrangements might be needed in practice to cover the highest risk layers.

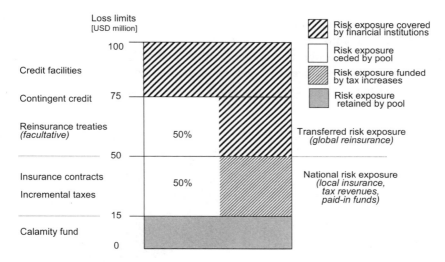

*Figure 9.7   Insurance Pool with Layered Risk-Transfer Structure -
Example*

The insurance pools can be managed in cooperation with private insurance companies, for example, by contracting them as sales agents and by outsourcing major operational tasks. The insurance companies could also be engaged as insurers of the lowest risk layer on a mutual basis to reduce issues of moral hazard associated with their agency role. It can be a complex process to evaluate opportunities in different risk-transfer and financing markets, but it is a task that should be pursued on an ongoing basis to ensure that the insurance vehicle continues to operate on optimal terms.

In most developed economies with significant exposures to catastrophe risks, public authorities are engaged in the establishment of insurance vehicles that often attract governmental support on a 'lender of last resort' basis. For example in the United States, the state authorities in Florida, California, and Hawaii have introduced special insurance programs to deal with major regional catastrophe exposures. Joint Underwriting Associations (JUA), the Florida Hurricane Catastrophe Fund (FHCF), the California Earthquake Authority (CEA), and the Hawaii Hurricane Relief Fund (HHRF) were established in the respective states after experiences with major catastrophe events.

The Hawaii Hurricane Relief Fund (HHRF) provides hurricane cover through participating insurance companies that exclude hurricane cover in their normal homeowner policies. The fund receives revenues from insurance premiums and property assessments by the insurance companies. The first 10% of losses are borne by the homeowners through deductibles with a higher layer covered by the insurers. The next level is reinsured in the market, and the top layer is covered by a line of credit secured by future surcharges on premiums (Figure 9.8).

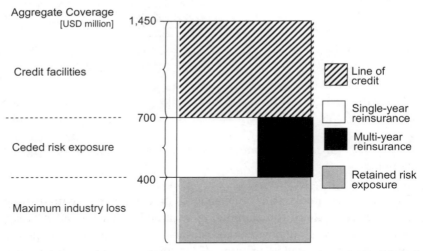

Figure 9.8   Insurance Cover of the Hawaii Hurricane Relief Fund (HHRF)

Similar insurance vehicles with comparable structures have been established in other exposed parts of the world including Europe and Asia. For example in Japan, the government owned Japanese Earthquake Reinsurance Company (JER) provides reinsurance for damages to residential property from earthquake and volcanic activities. JER in turn retrocedes part of its exposure to private insurance companies, while the government retains the rest of the aggregate exposure. The coverage in the Japanese earthquake reinsurance program is an example of a mixed structure that combines earned funds, reinsurance, and government commitments in different ways (Figure 9.9).

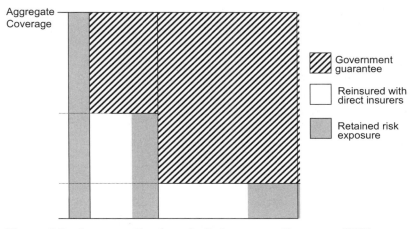

Figure 9.9   Japanese Earthquake Reinsurance Company (JER)

Conclusions

The establishment of different types of risk pooling vehicles can create additional insurance capacity for otherwise uninsurable catastrophe exposures in disaster prone countries. However, to maintain the economic efficiency of these vehicles, the essential managerial decisions should be commercially and actuarially based. This implies that claims are covered on predetermined contractual terms without any political interference. It also means that all surplus funds accumulated during the pool's operating life only can be used to pay claims associated with insured exposures. Hence, the insurance vehicles must be governed within an effective *legal and regulatory environment* that maintains a clear separation between government resources and the reserve funds maintained by the insurance pools. The catastrophe insurance vehicle, such as, an insurance pool, should outline a set of realistic risk management objectives in the initial phases of its establishment. Catastrophe exposures are theoretically infinitely large and, therefore, it could be prohibitively expensive to cover for all the highest loss layers associated with mega-catastrophes. Consequently, *affordability* is an important practical concern when an insurance vehicle is being introduced. This means that new insurance pools most likely would try to fund aggregate claims from events with up to say 100-year to 150-year return periods and probably no higher unless there are good economic rationales for it. The affordability of reinsurance coverage is obviously an essential determinant of the insurance premium the pool must charge, but it is important that the premiums are determined on an actuarial basis to ensure the financial sustainability of the insurance vehicles.

References

Bohn, J. G. and Hall, B. J. (1999). The Moral Hazard of Insuring the Insurers, in Froot, K. A. (Ed.) *The Financing of Catastrophe Risk*. The University of Chicago Press, Chicago.

Culp, C. L. (2001). The Risk Management Process: Business Strategy and Tactics. Wiley, New York.

Culp, C. L. (2002). The ART of Risk Management: Alternative Risk Transfer, Capital Structure, and the Convergence between Insurance and Capital Markets. Wiley, New York.

Cummins, J. D., Lewis, C. M. and Phillips, R. D. (1999). Pricing Excess-of-loss Reinsurance Contracts Against Catastrophic Loss, in Froot, K. A. (Ed.) *The Financing of Catastrophe Risk*. The University of Chicago Press, Chicago.

Freeman, P. K. and Martin, L. A. (2002). National systems for comprehensive disaster management: Financing reconstruction, Background Study Phase II. The Inter-American Development Bank, Washington, D.C.

Freeman, P. K., Martin, L. A., Mechler, R. and Warner, K. (2002). Catastrophes and development: Integrating natural catastrophes into development planning. Working Paper Series, Disaster Management Facility, The World Bank, Washington, D.C.

Froot, K.A. (1999). The Market for Catastrophe Risk: A Clinical Examination. National Bureau of Economic Research, Cambridge, MA.

Froot, K. A., Scharfstein, D. S. and Stein, J. C. (1994). A Framework for Risk Management. *Harvard Business Review*, 72(6), 91-102.

Guy Carpenter (2000). Managing the Financial Impacts of Natural Disaster Losses in Mexico: Government Options for Risk Financing & Risk Transfer, Latin America and the Caribbean Region. The World Bank, Washington, D.C.

Lester, R. and Gurenko, E. (2003). Financing Rapid Onset Natural Disaster Losses in India: A Risk Management Approach. Technical Paper, The World Bank, Washington, D.C.

Miller, K. D. (1998). Economic Exposure and Integrated Risk Management, *Strategic Management Journal*, 19, 497-514.

CHAPTER 10

Options Reasoning and Strategic Responsiveness: Discussion and Empirical Assessment

Torben Juul Andersen

Options related rationales are often used in strategy research and seem to imply that certain benefits can accrue from the adoption of real options analysis. Accordingly, this article suggests that an options perspective can be beneficial in the assessment of strategic decisions and argues that a predominant use in investment analyses should be linked to analyses of strategy formation. It further discusses different applications of the options perspective in strategy analyses and proposes that firm-specific strategic decision processes are needed to create strategic opportunities that lead to higher responsiveness and superior performance. Data from a cross-sectional industry study provides empirical evidence in support for these contentions.

Introduction
Two decades ago it was hinted that conventional cash flow analysis failed to capture the essence of strategic decision making while an options perspective might enhance analyses of investment decisions (Kester, 1984; Myers, 1984). Subsequently, option pricing theory was applied to analyze investment and capital budgeting decisions that incorporate different options related flexibilities (McDonald and Siegel, 1985, 1986; Kulatilaka and Marcus, 1988; Trigeorgis, 1988, 1993, 1995). The options perspective has also been used to analyze specific investment structures such as joint ventures (Kogut, 1991; Hurry, Miller and Bowman, 1992), global production networks (Kogut and Kulatilaka, 1994), and elements of the strategy making process (Bowman and Hurry, 1993; Sanchez, 1993). Even though the options perspective was considered 'pregnant with opportunity' for applications in the strategy field (Bettis, 1994) it has been difficult to

'deliver the baby' in practice (Adner and Levinthal, 2004; Busby and Pitts, 1997; Lander and Pinches, 1998; Coff and Laverty, 2001). Hence, a fundamental question arises whether the options perspective is useful in conceiving the strategic management process or invites limitations that are unattainable with effective strategy making.

The Options Perspective in Strategy-Making

The real options concept is rooted in the literature on derivative securities where the common option valuation models are derived on the basis of liquid markets for financial assets (Black and Scholes, 1973; Cox, Ross and Rubenstein, 1979). The finance field recognized the potential utility of real options analysis in other types of financial investment (Kester, 1984; Myers, 1984). A simple call option structure gives the holder the right to acquire an underlying asset at a predetermined price over a certain period of time (Hull, 1989). In an investment proposal, the underlying asset value is equivalent to the project's net present value and the strike price corresponds to the initial capital outlay. Since investment proposals typically build on firm-specific assets and capabilities, they constitute non-traded proposals referred to as real options as opposed to financial options. A given investment proposal can have several implicit call options that provide the firm with opportunities to start future business activities and optionalities may be ascribed to many types of flexibilities. Accordingly, the initial thrust was to adopt option pricing theory to the valuation of different option structures that could enhance the firm's flexibilities, e.g., in the form of growth, expansion, contraction, switching, deferral, and abandonment options, and develop a heuristic for the underlying investment decisions (McDonald and Siegel, 1985, 1986; Majd and Pindyck, 1987; Kulatilaka and Marcus, 1988; Copeland, Collar and Murrin, 1990; Smith and Nau, 1995). These contributions were further extended and integrated to support the firm's strategic investment and capital budgeting decisions (Dixit and Pindyck, 1994; Trigeorgis, 1995; Amram and Kulatilaka, 1999).

The real options associated with specific investments have been highlighted in management and international business studies. For example, joint ventures in new markets can be interpreted as option structures where limited initial capital outlays provide the venture partners with opportunities to develop capabilities that allow them to introduce future market activities, or possibly acquire the joint venture business (Hurry, Miller and Bowman, 1992; Chi and McGuire, 1996; Folta, 1998; Chi, 2000). Similarly, a cautious investment path, where additional funding only is committed after initial investments prove successful, constitutes a sequential abandonment option structure where the firm can halt expansion at different decision points if conditions become unfavorable (Andersen, 2000). Hence, small seed investments in foreign markets may be considered potential growth options while subsequent expansive investments can be structured as sequential entry into new market environments (Hurry, 1994; Chang, 1995, 1996). International manufacturing centers can also provide flexibilities that allow the firm to transfer production from relatively high cost areas to more cost effective locations in response to changes in foreign exchange rates and relative factor prices. Hence, a global operational network may constitute a portfolio of switching options that enhances the corporation's ability to manage its economic risk exposures (Kogut, 1991; Kogut and Kulatilaka, 1994). Furthermore, it has been suggested that resource committing strategic decisions can be managed as a portfolio of investment options that constitute the firm's strategic opportunities (Luehrman, 1998).

These predominant options approaches are generally supported by quantitative valuation techniques although there have been a few notable attempts to use the options perspective to conceptualize the general strategy formation process, or elements of it. Bowman and Hurry (1993) argued that real options as strategic opportunities are formed by finding and recombining existing assets and capabilities into viable alternative actions. Hence, an organization's resource base underpins a number of 'latent' options that must be recognized before they can be used to shape new business initiatives. Strategy evolves as the firm recognizes its inherent options and executes them over time. Some of these strategic opportunities constitute operational flexibilities while other optionalities allow the firm to make major shifts in its business activities and thereby adapt its strategic position to changing environmental conditions. Sanchez (1993, 1995) claimed that the firm should create flexibilities in the input and output markets along the firm's value chain configuration and optimize the value of the implied options portfolio. These options could represent product opportunities, new operating procedures, or alternative sourcing channels. Hence, the role of the strategic manager in this process would be to identify various flexibilities and build an options-set that provides the firm with maximum strategic maneuverability. McGrath (1997, 1999) used the options logic to analyze new business ventures and technology investment. She argued that entrepreneurial innovation requires high-variance environments while the subsequent irreversible investments

(The various contributions in the literature are presented in chronological order of publication)

Authors	Options perspective

Evaluation of real options in strategic investment decisions (*options exercise*)

Myers (1984)	Take growth options into account in capital budgeting
Kester (1984)	Analyze investment in future growth as call options
McDonald & Siegel (1985, 1986)	Estimating the value of the options to defer investment
Majd & Pindyck (1987)	The valuation and decision heuristic of the timing option
Kulatilaka & Marcus (1988)	General valuation of corporate real options
Copeland, Coller & Murrin (1990)	Investments as flexibility and abandonment options
He & Pindyck (1991)	Analyzing investment in flexible production capacity
Kemna (1993)	Adopting different option structures in investment decisions
Trigeorgis (1988, 1993, 1995)	Incorporating real options analysis in capital budgeting
Kulatilaka & Trigeorgis (1994)	Real options analysis of the flexibility to switch
Dixit & Pindyck (1994, 1995)	Advanced valuation techniques and decision heuristics
Smith & Nau (1995)	Using option pricing theory to value risky investment projects
Copeland & Keenan (1998)	Determining the value of flexibility in real strategic decisions
Kulatilaka & Perotti (1998)	Investment in growth options provide valuable opportunities
Slater, Reddy & Zwirlein (1998)	Options analysis as a tool to evaluate strategic investments
Amram & Kalatilaka (1999, 2000)	Real option pricing to value strategic investment decisions
Lint & Pennings (1999)	Strategic investment decisions as deferral and timing options
Leslie & Michaels (2000)	Apply real options analysis in strategic investment decisions
Copeland & Antikarov (2001)	Valuation of investment alternatives as different options

Managing different asset-based real options (*options maintenance*)

Kogut (1991)	Expanding through international joint ventures
Hurry, Miller & Bowman (1992)	Japanese investment in the United States as call options
Hurry (1994)	Shadow options as a global exploration strategy
Kogut & Kulatilaka (1994)	The value of a flexible global manufacturing network
Chang (1995, 1996)	Sequential market entry as international expansion strategy
Chi & McGuire (1996)	Using collaborative ventures as a mode of market entry
Mang (1998)	R&D investment as innovation options
Folta (1998)	Strategic alliances as real options
Luehrman (1998)	Strategy as a portfolio of real option investments
Chi (2000)	Options to acquire and divest joint venture investments

Real options recognition and strategic decision-making (*options creation*)

Bowman & Hurry (1993)	Strategy formation as a process of recognizing options
Sanchez (1993, 1995)	Strategic choice by acquiring value chain flexibilities
McGrath (1997, 1999)	Using options reasoning in technology development
Andersen (2000)	Development investment as sequential abandonment options

Table 10.1   Some Options Perspectives in Strategy Formation

associated with the commercialization of new innovations should be made when uncertainty has been sufficiently reduced. She also noted that uncertainties surrounding new business ventures such as technology risk, factor cost variability, changing demand conditions, etc., might be reduced by actively investing in knowledge enhancing activities.

These contributions in the literature outline somewhat differing perspectives of the options concept in strategy formation ranging from initial options creation to final options exercise (Table 1). It seems appropriate to separate the contributions in three categories according to their primary perspective. The bulk of the literature has emphasized valuation and decision heuristics in investment analyses (*exercise*). There has been some focus on the management of options embedded in specific asset structures (*maintenance*), whereas only a modest number of contributions have considered options recognition in strategy formation (*creation*). The literature review reveals an intense research focus around the use of option pricing theory and other quantitative methodologies to evaluate real options and guide investment decisions. In contrast, there have been limited efforts to apply the options perspective to the creation of options. While it is natural to focus on the options valuation techniques in initial applications of the options concept to strategic decision-making, options must nonetheless be recognized and created before they can play a strategic role. Therefore, it has been suggested that the option perspective should be adopted to analyze the entire 'options life cycle' from options creation to exercise. Certain option structures may be applicable to different cycle stages where abandonment options are particularly relevant in the analysis of development investment and deferral options in commercialization investment (Andersen, 2000). However, there remains an almost exclusive emphasis on options exercise and execution, whereas few contributions try to integrate the options perspective across the entire strategic management process.

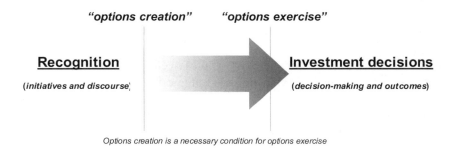

Figure 10.1 Strategy Formation as Real Option Management

Many practical applications of the options concept have adopted a valuation approach (Copeland and Keenan, 1998; Leslie and Michaels, 2000). To circumvent the seeming bias towards options exercise, it seems appropriate to direct more attention towards the organization's options creation process (Figure 10.1). Without an ability to recognize options within the organization there would be no strategic alternatives to analyze in the first place, i.e., the efficient creation of options constitutes an essential element of strategy formation.

The Performance Dynamic of Options

The ability to recognize the firm's latent options is a necessary condition for their subsequent exercise that not only increases the organization's operational agility but also allows the firm to change its strategic position (Bowman and Hurry, 1994). By establishing a high degree of flexibility in the firm's sourcing, manufacturing, and distribution channels it becomes easier to adapt the value chain configuration to changes in the external market environment (Sanchez, 1993, 1995). In other words, the organization's options creation capabilities may be intricately linked to the organization's strategic response capabilities (Bettis and Hitt, 1995). The existence of options is a prerequisite for flexible strategic maneuvering, i.e., the more strategic alternatives the organization can choose between, the higher is the chance that the firm can respond appropriately and with speed when the competitive environment changes. A high degree of adaptability is expected to be associated with better performance with organizational inertia being a common trait of performance laggards (Aldrich and Auster, 1986). Furthermore, if the organization is able to establish efficient and firm specific options creation capabilities it may form the basis for sustainable competitive advantage and generation of economic rents (Barney, 1997).

The options perspective promises to improve the prevailing strategic decision approaches (Damodaran, 2000). Commonly used discounted cash flow analyses often overlook the value associated with future growth opportunities embedded in business ventures and ignore some of the implicit timing flexibilities of strategic investments. These real options are potentially important because they provide the firm with opportunities to exploit strategic opportunities under favorable conditions without any commitment to exercise them if conditions turn unfavorable. Hence, firms with a palette of alternative strategic opportunities (real options) should be in a better position to avoid downside commercial risks while exploiting the upside business potentials promised by favorable changes in the market environment. This motivates the following hypothesis.

HYPOTHESIS 1: *The organization's options creation capabilities are positively associated with performance outcomes*

The flexibility embedded in real options has value and the theoretical value of the option depends on the level of uncertainty (volatility) ascribed to the net present value of the underlying business proposition (Dixit and Pindyck, 1994). The more the firm's strategic environment is exposed to uncertainty and unexpected change, the more diverse will be the expected payoffs from a given business opportunity. The real options that constitute new strategic opportunities have higher potential value in uncertain industry settings because the implied flexibility increases the firm's ability to start ventures under favorable conditions and avoid them altogether if circumstances are unfavorable. Hence, the flexibility associated with different options is deemed particularly advantageous to firm's that operate in dynamic environments (McGrath, 1997, 1999). This inspires the following hypothesis.

HYPOTHESIS 2: *The positive performance relationship of the organization's options creation capabilities is positively moderated in dynamic environments*

Despite the theoretical rationales of the options logic there is evidence suggesting that the proposed benefits fail to materialize. Surveys find that it still is uncommon among organizations to analyze the inherent option structures in a systematic manner (Busby and Pitts, 1997). Laboratory experiments indicate that subjective option valuations often vary considerably from their theoretical values (Howell and Jägle, 1997). In reality, managers seem to have limited understanding of the options concept and the potential use of different option pricing models (Lander and Pinches, 1998). An empirical study did not find the expected negative relationship between downside risk and option structures, such as, international joint ventures and multinational networks, as predicted by the options logic (Reuer and Leiblein, 2000). A variety of possible reasons are offered to explain possible performance shortfalls. For example, firms may simply fail to recognize the options they have, or they may lack appropriate management systems to monitor and exercise them appropriately. The

185

maintenance costs associated with the options, such as keeping parallel manufacturing capacities in different currency areas, may be substantial and prohibitive to positive performance. Furthermore, it is considered very difficult to integrate organizational capabilities that exploit the option structures, so the coordination costs associated with options exercise may be excessive. Coff and Laverty (2001) suggest that there is significant uncertainty about the investment's true value at the time of exercise, which makes the option valuation techniques hard to apply in practice. The options based firm arguably invests in knowledge that can be integrated into valuable capabilities (latent options) but there might be severe limitations in the organization's ability to transfer these competences into the development of viable business opportunities. All of these concerns indicate that organizational processes may exert a central influence on the effective development and utilization of the firm's options. Hence, an organization should adopt internal processes that induce efficient recognition and creation of options.

Strategy Processes and Options Creation Capabilities

Several scholars predict positive outcome effects from the options approach to strategy making (Barney, 1997; McGrath, 1997) but their prediction is challenged by potential shortcomings in the organization. These shortcomings include uncertainty avoidance and conflict of preferences (Cyert and March, 1963), internal complexity (Hannan and Freeman, 1984), limiting path dependencies (Dierickx and Cool, 1989), organizational inertia (Aldrich and Auster, 1986), etc. The strategy field has outlined two major elements of the complex strategy formation processes, strategic planning and strategic emergence, that arguably may curtail some of these inhibiting organizational characteristics and thereby furnish potential options advantages. The planning, or strategic management, approach argues that use of systematic and rational analyses can help identify new opportunities while furnishing creative strategic thinking. It is also argued that important strategic actions can arise from initiatives taken among managers deep within the organization. Hence, both strategy-making modes may support the organization's options creation capabilities.

Strategy-making does not necessarily reflect intended actions but may comprise important managerial actions taken in response to emerging events (Mintzberg, 1978; Mintzberg and Waters, 1985). New business initiatives can emerge from decisions made by managers dispersed throughout the organization (Mintzberg, 1994). Bower

(1982) identified the importance of such resource-committing actions as they develop the capabilities that eventually shape the firm's strategic options (Noda and Bower, 1996). Decentralization of decision power allows lower-level managers to take initiatives that subsequently may constitute viable choices senior management can make for the firm's formal strategy (Burgelman, 1988). Hence, strategic emergence can arise within a decentralized decision structure where managers have authority to take independent actions that furnish experimentation and options creation. Effective options creation capabilities are conceivably associated with a firm's ability to learn through information processing that allows the firm to do new things and in ways it was unable to pursue before (Huber, 1991). Options creation also resonates with the concept of dynamic capabilities, which constitutes the organization's ability to create new useful competencies in response to changing market conditions (Lei, Hitt and Bettis, 1996; Teece, Pisano and Shuen, 1997). These rationales suggest the following hypothesis.

HYPOTHESIS 3: *Strategy formation through emergence has a positive association with the organization's options creation capabilities*

The strategic management paradigm prescribes an analytical strategy formation process that encompasses environmental analysis, strategy formulation, implementation, evaluation, and control (Schendel and Hofer, 1979). This rational strategy approach was motivated by a need for systematic analysis in response to the increasingly dynamic market conditions. This type of strategic planning was typically seen as a way to facilitate discussions of needed strategic actions, integrate internal competencies, and coordinate responsive actions (Grynier et al., 1986; Lorange and Vancil, 1995, 1977). The planning process may encourage adaptive strategic thinking and support the search for new business opportunities (Rhyne, 1986; Ansoff, 1988; Miller and Cardinal, 1994). Hence, the strategic management process may furnish the creative thinking and internal coordination of competencies required to develop new options. This inspires the following hypothesis.

HYPOTHESIS 4: *Strategy formation through planning has a positive association with the organization's options creation capabilities*

Torben Juul Andersen

In the new competitive landscape, effective organizations are characterized by intense use of communication technologies and decentralized management approaches (Bettis and Hitt, 1995). A decentralized decision structure combined with information technology enhanced communication that facilitates the recombination of existing competencies can support innovation and organizational learning processes (Huber, 1990, 1991; Kogut and Zander, 1992). Information systems and computer networks improve the organization's ability to exchange information among managers and ease access to essential distributed data sources. This type of computer-mediated communication can support absorptive capacity that allows the organization to identify new opportunities and coordinate them internally (Cohen and Levinthal, 1990). The effective communication among dispersed managers can also help an organization become more innovative (Zuboff, 1989; Huber 1990). Hence, computer-mediated communication may support the decentralized strategic decision structure that underpins the organization's options creation capabilities. This argues for the following hypothesis.

HYPOTHESIS 5: *The positive association between strategic emergence and the organization's options creation capabilities is positively moderated by computer-mediated communication*

It is argued that a prime role of the strategic planning process is to coordinate organizational actions and integrate internal competencies (Grynier et al., 1986; Lorange and Vancil; 1995, 1977). Hence, computer-mediated communication among the managers located in different parts of the firm may facilitate the organization's integrative efforts and accommodate creative discussions. There has been some evidence that computer-based communication systems can support the planning process (DeSanctis and Jackson, 1994). This leads to the following hypothesis.

HYPOTHESIS 6: *The positive association between strategic planning and the organization's options creation capabilities is positively moderated by computer-mediated communication*

The hypothesized relationships are illustrated in Figure 10.2.

Methodology

To investigate the model across organizations facing different levels of uncertainty in their strategic environments, several distinct industries were identified. Strategic uncertainty was approximated initially by the standard error of the regression slope coefficients of the 10-year time-series on net sales and operating income across four-digit SIC industries included in Compustat (Keats and Hitt, 1988). This analysis identified various industries with different levels of uncertainty ranging from industries in consumer goods (meat packing, flour, cereals, sugar products, beverages, clothing, and furniture) in the lower end of the uncertainty spectrum to computer products industries (computers, storage devises, calculators, and measuring instruments) representing higher levels of uncertainty. A sample of 222 organizations was extracted from the identified industries. The proposed model constructs were subsequently measured on the basis of responses solicited from the senior executives in charge of the market-oriented functions in each of the 222 organizations.

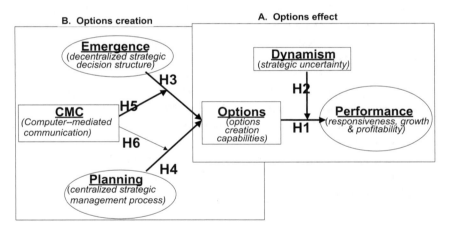

Note: The 'fat' lines indicate relationships supported by the empirical data.

Figure 10.2 A Real Options Model of Strategy Formation

Emergent strategy is characterized by dispersed strategic decision power and was assessed on the basis of Aiken and Hage's measure of decision authority (Dewar, Whetten and Boje, 1980). The items were modified to represent strategy-making issues, e.g., new market activities, product development, changes in practices and policies, etc. (Miller, 1987). Emergence indicates the extent to which the managers

189

reporting to the executive board are authorized to take initiatives on their own. Planning reflects the organization's adherence to the strategic management process (Schendel and Hofer, 1979). Strategic planning was measured on the basis of previously tested items indicating the firm's emphasis on key elements of the planning process, e.g., mission statement, long-term plans and goals, action plans, and evaluation (Boyd and Reuning-Elliott, 1998). Computer-mediated communication captures the managers' use of information technology and electronic networks to facilitate internal communication. This was measured as the extent to which managers use different computer-based networks to exchange information and access data across the organization's functional areas (Kettinger and Grover, 1997; Andersen, 2001). The options creation capabilities indicate the organization's ability to innovate, nurture, and utilize concrete business opportunities in response to the risks represented in an uncertain and changing environment (Boer, 2002). Options creation reflects the extent to which the organization generates suggestions, converts them to new strategic opportunities, and changes the way things are done (Bowman and Hurry, 1993; Huber, 1991; McGrath, 1997). A firm specific self-reported dynamism measure was also derived to capture the level of uncertainty in the organization's strategic environment. The measure indicates changes in the firm's product profitability and the need for product development and changes in internal procedures (Miller, 1987). Finally, performance was measured by three self-assessed indicators of the firm's responsiveness to environmental change, sales growth, and profitability compared to its close competitors (Dess and Robinson, 1984; Bettis and Hitt, 1995). The appendix provides an overview of the items adopted in the questionnaire.

Results

Useable questionnaires were returned from 110 of the 222 solicited organizations corresponding to a response rate of 49.5%. The questionnaires were tested for non-response biases, and no differences in assets, sales, growth, return, or profit margin were identified. The reliability of respondents was validated through comparison between the self-reported measures on growth and profitability and archival performance data derived from Compustat. The correlation coefficient between the archival and subjective measures on sales growth was 0.42 and 0.49 on the profitability measures. The correlation coefficients calculated across the sampled firms within each of the four-digit SIC industries ranged between 0.45 and 0.60. These results were deemed favorable compared to previous research (Dess and Robinson, 1984). The reliability of the executives was tested further in 10% of the sample by comparison to secondary respondents. The average inter-rater reliability between the primary and secondary respondents was 0.70, which was considered satisfactory (Rosenthal and Rosnow, 1984). Finally, the model constructs were tested for internal consistency by performing factor analysis on all item responses where items clearly loaded on separate factors consistent with the proposed model constructs.

Table 10.2 provides descriptive statistics and correlation coefficients on the sample. As it appears, options have significant correlation coefficients with emergence, planning, and computer-mediated communication (CMC), i.e., there are positive relationships between the firms' strategy processes and options creation capabilities. Furthermore, options have significant correlation coefficients to responsiveness, growth, and profitability, i.e., there is a positive relationship between the firms' options creation capabilities and organizational performance. The alphas calculated on the emergence, planning, computer-mediated communication (CMC), and options measures amounted to 0.75, 0.82, 0.81, and 0.71, which was deemed satisfactory (Nunnally and Bernstein, 1994).

(n=110)	Mean	S.D.	1	2	3	4	5	6
1 Emergence	13.64	4.29	-	-	-	-	-	-
2 Planning	17.37	4.92	0.117	-	-	-	-	-
3 CMC	11.43	3.17	0.244**	0.155+	-	-	-	-
4 Options	7.10	1.83	0.245**	0.371**	0.201*	-	-	-
5 Response	3.54	0.89	-0.023	0.167+	0.096	0.235*	-	-
6 Growth	3.73	1.34	0.235*	0.341**	0.105	0.366**	0.257**	-
7 Profitability	3.72	1.29	0.122	0.408**	0.202*	0.343**	0.249**	0.608**

+ $p < 0.10$; * $p < 0.05$; ** $p < 0.01$

Table 10.2 Descriptive Data and Correlation Coefficients

The hypotheses were tested on the basis of multiple regression analyses including interaction terms (Aiken and West, 1991). First, regressions with performance as the dependent variable, and options, and the interaction with dynamism as independent variables tested hypotheses 1 and 2. Regressions with options as the dependent variable, and the strategy constructs, computer-mediated communication, and their interactions as independent variables tested hypotheses 3, 4, 5 and 6. Organizational size often confounds performance effects and was therefore included as control variable in the first regression analysis. The performance measures (responsiveness, growth, and profitability) were assessed in relation to the firms' close competitors to eliminate effects from differences in returns across industries. The sample consisted of single business firms and was therefore not influenced by corporate strategy effects. The independent variables and interaction terms used in the regression analyses were tested for potential multicollinearity effects. The variance inflation factors were well below 9.5 and hence did not indicate any problems (Kleinbaum, Kupper, Muller and Nizam, 1998). The error terms of the multiple regressions were checked for outliers, heteroscedasticity, and normality.

The first regression analysis shows a significant positive relationship between options and the three performance measures of responsiveness, growth, and profitability (Table 10.3). This provides support for hypothesis 1.

(n=110)	(*Standardized Regression Coefficients*)					
Dependent variable:	Responsiveness		Sales Growth		Profitability	
Options	.224*	.242**	.244**	.270**	.200*	.223*
Emergence	-.084	-.099	.162+	.090	-.029	-.085
Planning	.087	.094	.211*	.213*	.309**	.312**
Ln assets	.066	.009	-.002	-.016	.230**	.216*
Dynamism	-	-.050	-	-.033	-	-.037
Options by dynamism	-	.147	-	.259**	-	.208*
Multiple R^2	.261	.301	.447	.513	.508	.547
Adjusted R^2	.068	.093	.170	.219	.230	.259
F-significance	.099	.114	.000	.000	.000	.000

$^+ p < 0.10$; $^* p < 0.05$; $^{**} p < 0.01$

Table 10.3   Multiple Regression Analysis (Options Effects)

Furthermore, the interaction term between options and dynamism indicates that the relationship between the firm's options creation capabilities and both sales growth and profitability is significantly higher in environments characterized by dynamic change. These results provide partial support for hypothesis 2. The second regression analysis shows significant positive relationships between options and the two strategy-making processes of emergence and planning (Table 10.4). These results provide support for hypothesis 3 and 4. Furthermore, there is a significant positive relationship between options and the interaction term between emergence and computer-mediated communication. This supports hypothesis 5. However, there is no apparent relationship between options and the interaction between planning and computer-mediated communication, i.e., there is no support for hypothesis 6.

(n=110)	(*Standardized Regression Coefficients*)		
Dependent variable:	Strategic Opportunities (Options)		
Emergence	.207**	.160*	.147^{+}
Planning	.344**	.308**	.304**
CMC	-	.117	.132
Emergence by CMC	-	.161*	.160*
Planning by CMC	-	-	.067
Multiple R^2	.429	.464	.469
Adjusted R^2	.168	.186	.182
F-significance	.000	.000	.000

$^{+}$ $p < 0.10$; * $p < 0.05$; ** $p < 0.01$

Table 10.4   Multiple Regression Analysis (Options Creation)

Discussion

The results provide initial evidence that the organization's application of particular strategy making modes has a positive influence on the ability to create options. The firm's options creation capabilities, in turn, are positively associated with performance particularly in dynamic environments. The firms' options creation capabilities seem to be supported by the two strategy-making modes of strategic emergence, embedded in a decentralized strategic decision making process, and strategic planning, reflected in a centralized analytical strategic management process. The relationship between strategic emergence and the organization's options creation capabilities seems to be significantly enhanced by computer-mediated communication between managers located in different parts of the firm. Interestingly, we do not find any effect on the use of computer-mediated communication in the strategic planning process as suggested by other studies (DeSanctis and Jackson, 1994). One reason could be that the planning process entails rich conversations with a high content of tacit knowledge that is more difficult to communicate electronically. In contrast, the quality of decentralized decision making processes may benefit from cross-functional links and organization wide data access supported by computerized communication systems (Huber, 1990). The findings support the asserted importance of specific strategy-making modes to induce options creation capabilities. Whereas it might be opportune to have an extensive options portfolio with a high theoretical market value, what really matters might be the organization's ability to create options effectively in a dynamic environment. In other words, the ability to evaluate and decide about the exercise of existing options is not a sufficient condition for excess performance. It is equally important to have the capabilities that allow the firm to create options in response to changing environmental conditions.

Reuer and Leiblein (2000) questioned the benefits that may accrue from commonly recognized option structures. They suggested that options embedded in multinational networks may increase organizational complexity and coordination cost so much that any potential benefits could be reversed. Similarly, Coff and Laverty (2001) argued that the integration of capabilities in options creation is difficult and depends on effective organizational communication, interaction, and coordination efforts. They observed a lack of options creation capabilities that could lead to suboptimal outcomes. These arguments, combined with other empirical evidence on the shortcomings of the current use of the options perspective in strategic decision making (Busby and Pitts, 1997; Howell and Jägle, 1997; Lander and Pinches, 1998), reaffirms the significance of effective options creation in the strategy formation process. The current study sheds further light on this central issue by showing that the organization's options creation capabilities seem to matter, and that particular strategy-making modes have a positive influence on options creation. Furthermore, use of information technology as a facilitator of organizational communication has a positive moderating effect on the organization's options creation capabilities. These results are consistent with observations of contemporary management practices characterized by decentralized decision structure and intense use of new communication technologies (e.g., Bettis and Hitt, 1995). They focus our attention on the importance of specific strategy-making modes as effective ways to develop options that increase the firm's strategic maneuverability and action space.

Previous empirical studies have primarily considered options reflected in multinational structure, joint venture investment, and operational flexibilities. This approach captures specific option structures but does not capture how the options were created and developed in the firm's strategy formation process. In contrast, the options construct introduced in this exploratory study reflects the ability to create options by identifying new ways of doing things, convert them into actionable strategic opportunities that allow the firm to change the way things are done. This measure incorporates elements of learning, innovation, and dynamic capabilities (Lei, Hitt and Bettis, 1996; Teece, Pisano and Shuen, 1997). Options are created by recognizing the firm's existing capabilities and recombining them into new competencies that provide opportunities to change and adapt the firm's strategic position (Kogut and Zander, 1992; Bowman and Hurry, 1993). There is obviously room for further refinement of the option measures in future strategy research, and there may be a need to distinguish more clearly between options creation and options exercise to enable a more holistic analysis of the options perspective in the complex strategy formation process.

Conclusions

This paper argues for an increased focus on the organization's options creation capabilities, and an exploratory study indicates that the ability to create options seem to be induced by specific strategy making modes, and options in turn are associated with higher performance. These results have several implications. First, options creation capabilities, and hence the firm's ability to identify and develop actionable opportunities, do appear to make a difference to performance particularly in dynamic environments. Second, it is not enough to support the exercise of existing options with a theoretical decision heuristic since the firm's inherent options may be unable to provide sufficient responsiveness. Different strategy-making modes may induce the creation of options that are more responsive to current environmental conditions. The study indicates that both strategic emergence in the form of a decentralized strategic decision making process, and strategic planning, in the form of a centralized analytical strategic management process, can support the organization's options creation capabilities. Furthermore, the options creation from strategic emergence can be supported by computer-enhanced communication. The results are interesting because they indicate that options creation capabilities do seem to have significant performance effects that are induced by specific strategy-making modes. This should inspire a more holistic approach to the options concept in strategy research with equal emphasis on options creation and options exercise and further analyses of the organizational processes that may enhance the efficiencies of these important elements of the options perspective.

References

Adner, R. and Levinthal, D. A. (2004). What is not a real option: Considering boundaries for the application of real options to business strategy. *Academy of Management Review*, 29(1), 74-85.

Aiken, L. A. and West, S. G. (1991). *Multiple Regression: Testing and Interpreting Interactions*. Sage, Newbury Park.

Aldrich, H., and Auster, E. (1986). Even dwarfs started small: Liabilities of age and size and their strategic implications, in Staw, B. and Cummings, L. L. (Eds.), *Research in Organizational Behavior*, VIII. JAI Press, Connecticut.

Amram, M. and Kulatilaka, N. (1999a). *Real Options: Managing Strategic Investment in an Uncertain World*. Harvard Business School Press, Boston.

Amram M. and Kulatilaka, N. (1999b). Disciplined decisions: Aligning strategy with the financial markets. *Harvard Business Review*, 77(1), 95-104.

Andersen, T. J. (2000). Real options analysis in strategic decision making: An applied approach in a dual options framework. *Journal of Applied Management Studies*, 9, 235-255.

Andersen, T. J. (2001). Information technology, strategic decision making approaches and organizational performance in different industrial settings. *Journal of Strategic Information Systems*, 10, 101-119.

Ansoff, H. I. (1988). *The New Corporate Strategy*. Wiley, New York.

Barney, J. B. (1997). *Gaining and Sustaining Competitive Advantage*. Prentice-Hall, Upper Sadle River, NJ.

Bettis, R.A. (1994). Commentary: Shadow options and global exploration strategies, in Shrivastava, P., Huff, A. and Dutton, J. (eds.) *Advances in Strategic Management*, 10A, 249-253.

Bettis, R. A. and Hitt, M. A. (1995). The new competitive landscape. *Strategic Management Journal*, Special Issue, 16, 7-19.

Black, F. and Scholes, M. (1973). The pricing of options and corporate liabilities, *Journal of Political Economy*, 81, 637-654.

Boer, F. P. (2002). *The Real Options Solution: Finding Total Value in a High-Risk World.* Wiley, New York.

Bowman, E.H., and D. Hurry (1993). Strategy through the options lens: an integrated view of resource investments and the incremental-choice process. *Academy of Management Review*, 18, 760-782.

Bower, J. L. (1982). *Managing the resource allocation process.* Harvard Business School Press, Boston (First published in 1970).

Boyd, B. K. and Reuning-Elliott, E. (1998). A measurement model of strategic planning. *Strategic Management Journal*, 19, 181-192.

Burgelman, R. A. (1988). Strategy making as a social learning process: The case of internal corporate venturing. *Interfaces*, 18, 74-85.

Busby, J. S. and Pitts, C. G. C. (1997). Real options in practice: An exploratory survey of how finance officers deal with flexibility in capital appraisal. *Management Accounting Research*, 8, 169-186.

Chang, S.L. (1995). International expansion strategy of Japanese firms: capabilities building through sequential entry. *Academy of Management Journal*, 38, 383-407.

Chang, S.J. (1996). An evolutionary perspective on diversification and corporate restructuring: entry, exit, and economic performance during 1981-89. *Strategic Management Journal*, 17, 587-611.

Chi, T. L. (2000). Options to acquire and divest a joint venture. *Strategic Management Journal*, 21, 665-687.

Chi, T. L. and McGuire, D. J. (1996). Collaborative ventures and value of learning: integrating the transaction cost and strategic option perspectives on the choice of market entry modes. *Journal of International Business Studies*, 27, 285-307.

Coff, R. W. and Laverty, K. J. (2001). Dilemmas in exercise decisions for real options on core competencies. Paper presented at the Academy of Management Conference, Washington DC.

Cohen, W. M. and Levinthal, D. A. (1990). Absorptive capacity: A new perspective on learning and innovation. *Administrative Science Quarterly*, 35, 128-152.

Copeland, T. E., Coller, T. and Murrin, J. (1990). *Valuation: Measuring and Managing the Value of Companies*. Wiley, New York.

Copeland, T. E. and Keenan, P. T. (1998a). How much is flexibility worth? *McKinsey Quarterly*, (2), 38-49.

Copeland, T. E. and Keenan, P. T. (1998b). Making real options real. *McKinsey Quarterly*, (3), 128-141.

Cox, J. C., Ross, S. A. and Rubinstein, M. (1979). Option pricing: A simplified approach. *Journal of Financial Economics*, 7, 229-263.

Cyert, R. M. and March, J. G. (1963). *A Behavioral Theory of the Firm*. Prentice-Hall, Englewood Cliffs, NJ.

Damodaran, A. (2000). The promise of real options. *Journal of Applied Corporate Finance*, 13(2), 29-44.

DeSanctis, G. and Jackson, B. M. (1994). Coordination of information technology management: Team-based structures and computer-based communication systems. *Journal of Management Information Systems*, 10, 85-110.

Dewar, R. D., Whetten, D. A. and Boje, D. (1980). An examination of the reliability and validity of the Aiken & Hage scales of centralization, formalization, and task routines. *Administrative Science Quarterly*, 25, 120-128.

Dierickx, I. and Cool, K. (1989). Asset stock accumulation and sustainability of competitive advantage. *Management Science*, 35, 1504-1514.

Dixit, A. and Pindyck, R. S. (1994). *Investment Under Uncertainty*, Princeton University Press, New Jersey.

Dess, G. G. and Robinson, R. B. (1984). Measuring organizational performance in the absence of objective measures: The case of the privately-held firm and conglomerate business unit. *Strategic Management Journal*, 5, 265-273.

Folta, T. B. (1998). Governance and uncertainty: The tradeoff between administrative control and commitment. *Strategic Management Journal*, 19, 1007-1028.

Hannan, M. T. and Freeman, J. (1984). Structural inertia and organizational change. *American Sociological Review*, 49, 149-164.

Howell, S. D. and Jägle, A. J. (1997). Laboratory evidence on how managers intuitively value real growth options. *Journal of Business Finance and Accounting*, 24, 915-935.

Huber, G. P. (1990). A theory of the effects of advanced information technologies on organization design, intelligence, and decision making. *Academy of Management Review*, 15, 47-71.

Huber, G. P. (1991). Organizational learning: The contributing processes and the literatures. *Organization Science*, 2, 88-115.

Hull, J. C. (1989). *Options, Futures, & Other Derivatives*. Prentice-Hall, Upper Saddle River, NJ.

Hurry D., Miller, A.T. and Bowman, E. H. (1992). Calls on high-technology: Japanese exploration of venture capital investment in the United States. *Strategic Management Journal*, 13, 85-101.

Hurry, D. (1994). Shadow options and global exploration strategies, in Shrivastava, P., Huff, A. and Dutton, J. (eds.) *Advances in Strategic Management*, 10A, 229-248.

Keats, B. and Hitt, M. A. (1988). A causal model of linkages among environmental dimensions, macro organizational characteristics, and performance. *Academy of Management Journal*, 31, 570-598.

Kester, W. C. (1984). Today's options for tomorrow's growth. *Harvard Business Review*, 62(2), 153-160.

Kettinger, W. J., and Grover, V. (1997). The use of computer-mediated communication in an interorganizational context. *Decision Sciences*, 28, 513-555.

Kleinbaum, D. G., Kupper, L. K., Muller, K. E. and Nizam, A. (1998). *Applied Regression Analysis and Other Multivariate Methods*. Third Edition. Duxbury Press, Pacific Grove, CA.

Kogut, B. and Zander, U. (1992). Knowledge of the firm, combinative capabilities, and the replication of technology. *Organization Science*, 3, 383-397.

Kogut, B. (1991). Joint ventures and the option to expand and acquire. *Management Science*, 37, 19-33.

Kogut, B. and Kulatilaka, N. (1994a). Operating flexibility, global manufacturing and the option value of a multinational network. *Management Science*, 40, 123-138.

Kogut, B. and Kulatilaka, N. (1994b). Options thinking and platform investments: Investing in opportunity. *California Management Review*, 36(2), 52-71.

Kulatilaka, N. and Marcus, A. J. (1988). General formulation of corporate real options. *Research in Finance*, 7, 183-199.

Kulatilaka, N. and Trigeorgis, L. (1994). The general flexibility to switch: Real options revisited. *International Journal of Finance*, 6, 778-798.

Lander, D. M. and Pinches (1998). Challenges to the Practical Implementation of Modeling and Valuing Real Options. *The Quarterly Review of Economics and Finance*, 38, 537-561.

Lei, M., Hitt, A. and Bettis, R. A. (1996). Dynamic core competencies through meta-learning and strategic context. *Journal of Management*, 22, 549-569.

Leslie, K. J. and Michaels, M. P. (2000). The real power of real options. *McKinsey Quarterly*, (3), 1-6.

Lorange, P. and Vancil, R. F. (1995). How to design a strategic planning system, in Lorange, P. *Strategic Planning and Control: Issues in the Strategy Process*. Blackwell, Cambridge, MA (First published in 1976).

Luehrman, T. A. (1998a). Investment opportunities as real options: Getting started on the numbers. *Harvard Business Review,* 76(4), 51-67.
Luehrman, T. A. (1998b). Strategy as a portfolio of real options. *Harvard Business Review*, 76(5), 89-99.

Majd, S. and Pindyck, R. (1987). Time to build, option value, and investment decisions. *Journal of Financial Economics*, 18, 7-27.

McDonald, R. L. and Siegel, D. R. (1985). Investment and valuation of firms when there is an option to shut down. *International Economic Review*, 26, 331-349.

McDonald, R. L. and Siegel, D. R. (1986). The value of waiting to invest. *Quarterly Journal of Economics*, 101, 707-728.

McGrath, R.G. (1997). A real options logic for initiating technology positioning investments. *Academy of Management Review*, 22, 974-996.

McGrath, R.G. (1999). Falling forward: Real options reasoning and entrepreneurial failure. *Academy of Management Review*, 24, 13-30.

Miller, D. (1987). The structural and environmental correlates of business strategy. *Strategic Management Journal*, 8, 55-76.

Miller, C. C., and Cardinal, L. B. (1994). Strategic planning and firm performance: A synthesis of more than two decades of research. *Academy of Management Journal*, 37, 1649-1665.

Mintzberg, H. and Waters, J. E. (1985). Of strategies, deliberate and emergent. *Strategic Management Journal*, 6, 257-272.

Myers, S.C. (1984). Finance theory and financial strategy. *Interfaces*, January-February, 126-137.

Noda, T., and Bower, J. L. (1996). Strategy making as iterated processes of resource allocation. *Strategic Management Journal*, 17, 159-192.

Nunnally, J. C., and Bernstein, I. H. (1994). *Psychometric Theory*. Third Edition. McGraw-Hill, New York.

Price, J. L. (1972). *Handbook of Organizational Measurement*. Heath, Lexington, MA.

Reuer, J. J. and Leiblein, M. J. (2000). Downside risk implications of multinationality and international joint ventures. *Academy of Management Journal*, 43, 203-214.

Rhyne, L. C. (1986). The relationship of strategic planning to financial performance. *Strategic Management Journal*, 7, 423-436.

Rosenthal, R. and Rosnow, R. L. (1984). *Essentials of Behavioral Research: Methods and Data Analysis*. McGraw-Hill, New York.

Sanchez, R. (1993). Strategic flexibility, firm organization, and managerial work in dynamic markets: a strategic options perspective, in Shrivastava, P., Huff, A. and Dutton, J. (eds.) *Advances in Strategic Management*, 9, JAI Press, Connecticut.

Sanchez, R. (1995). Strategic flexibility in product competition. *Strategic Management Journal*, Special Issue, 16, 135-159.

Schendel, D. and Hofer, C. (1979). *Strategic Management: a new view of business policy and planning*. Little Brown, Boston.

Smith, J. E. and Nau, R. F. (1995). Valuing risky projects: Option pricing theory and decision analysis. *Management Science*, 41, 795-816.

Teece, D, J., Pisano, G. and Shuen, A. (1997). Dynamic capabilities and strategic management. *Strategic Management Journal*, 18, 509-533.

Trigeorgis, L. (1988). A conceptual options framework for capital budgeting. *Advances in Futures and Options Research*, 3, 145-167.

Trigeorgis, L. (1993). The nature of option interactions and the valuation of investments with multiple real options. *Journal of Financial and Quantitative Analysis*, 28, 1-20.

Trigeorgis, L. (1996). *Real Options: Managerial Flexibility and Strategic Resource Allocation*. MIT Press, Cambridge, MA.

Zuboff, S. (1988). *In the Age of the Smart Machine*. Basic Books, New York.

Appendix

Items adopted in the questionnaire

Emergence - *Decentralized strategic decision structure*
- The extent to which managers can start important market activities without top management approval
- The extent to which managers can market to new customer segments without approval from top management
- The extent to which managers can initiate new product and service developments without top management approval
- The extent to which managers can introduce new practices without approval from top management
- The extent to which managers can develop new internal capabilities without top management approval

Planning- *Centralized strategic management process*
- The emphasis the organization puts on the development of a mission statement
- The emphasis the organization puts on long-term plans
- The emphasis the organization puts on annual goals
- The emphasis the organization puts on short-term action plans
- The emphasis the organization puts on on-going evaluations of strategic objectives

CMC - *Computer-mediated communication*
- The extent to which managers use electronic mail to communicate across the organization
- The extent to which managers access information from other parts of the organization via the computer network
- The extent to which managers use electronic means to exchange information with managers in other functional areas

Strategic Opportunities (Options) - *Options creation capabilities*
- The extent to which suggestions to do things differently arise in the organization
- The extent to which ideas about customer and product developments are converted into business opportunities
- The extent to which the way work is done is being changed in the organization

Dynamism - *Strategic uncertainty*
- The extent to which profitability of different products has changed over the past five years
- The importance of identifying new customers and developing products and services
- The importance of changing practices and developing new internal capabilities

Performance – *Responsiveness/ Sales growth/ Profitability*
- The organization's ability to sense environmental change, and effectively respond to it, compared to close competitors
- The organization's position relative to close competitors over the past three years - growth in net sales
- The organization's position relative to close competitors over the past three years - profitability (ROA)